PRAISE FOR *THE UNSTUCK CHURCH*

Your church is perfectly designed to get the results you are currently getting. If you're satisfied with the results, write a book. If not, read this one . . . with your entire leadership team. *The Unstuck Church* is disruptive and instructional. Before you finish the first chapter, you'll understand why my friend Tony Morgan is one of the most sought-after church consultants in the nation.

ANDY STANLEY
SENIOR PASTOR
NORTH POINT MINISTRIES

Tony Morgan has written a practical, timely, and important book every pastor and church leader should read. In *The Unstuck Church* Tony shares years of ministry leadership experience about the life cycles of churches. Whether you are a part of a church plant or a 100-year-old established church, there is a wealth of wisdom in this book for you. If you care about your church, take your team through this book.

CRAIG GROESCHEL
PASTOR OF LIFE.CHURCH AND AUTHOR OF
DIVINE DIRECTION: 7 DECISIONS THAT WILL CHANGE YOUR LIFE

Every once in a while you find a book that makes you ask, "Where has this been all my (ministry) life?" This is one of those books. *The Unstuck Church* functions as a mirror. Whether you're planting, growing, plateaued, declining, or dying, you'll see yourself accurately, sometimes painfully so. But more than that, Tony gives you the practical advice you need to help get you unstuck.

CAREY NIEUWHOF
FOUNDING AND TEACHING PASTOR
CONNEXUS CHURCH

In *The Unstuck Church: Equipping Churches to Experience Sustained Health*, my friend Tony Morgan draws on his experience as founder and lead strategist for The Unstuck Group, a team that helps churches of every size and shape grow and thrive. Exploring the life cycle of every church, Tony reveals what's needed in each stage for churches to serve fully as God intends. Whether you're launching a new church or seeking remedies for your congregation's challenges, this book provides biblical wisdom drawn from firsthand, heartfelt experience. Highly recommended!

CHRIS HODGES

SENIOR PASTOR, CHURCH OF THE HIGHLANDS

AUTHOR OF *FRESH AIR* AND *THE DANIEL DILEMMA*

In each generation God raises up gifted, courageous leaders who speak and write prophetically and strategically. Tony Morgan is one of these leaders in our generation. His love and belief for the church is more than clear in his new book. He calls us to refuse to accept mediocrity and rise up in this hour to recommit ourselves to dynamic growth both spiritually and numerically.

DR. RONNIE FLOYD

SENIOR PASTOR, CROSS CHURCH

IMMEDIATE PAST PRESIDENT,

SOUTHERN BAPTIST CONVENTION

Church leaders, it doesn't matter if your church is big or small, experiencing success or stuck, Tony Morgan's new book is a resource you need *now*. *The Unstuck Church* strikes the perfect balance of comprehensive insight and concise, practical help. I love how Tony leverages his passion for the local church and his ministry experience to help our churches get healthy and grow.

SHANE DUFFEY

EXECUTIVE PASTOR

NEWSPRING CHURCH

"Yes! Yes! Yes!" was my reaction to reading *The Unstuck Church*. Tony Morgan is one of the best strategic leaders serving churches today, and in this book you'll see why. Tony's experience working with hundreds of churches will equip you with the wisdom and confidence to lead well whether your church is growing, steady, or stuck. I'll be recommending this book to every church leader I know.

JENNI CATRON
FOUNDER OF THE 4SIGHT GROUP AND AUTHOR OF
THE 4 DIMENSIONS OF EXTRAORDINARY LEADERSHIP

Tony has encouraged me in my leadership and challenged my thinking for many years. *The Unstuck Church* is no exception. Tony takes years of experience helping churches around the world and translates the wisdom he's gained into practical next steps to help our churches sustain health and growth. This book is a gift to the church at large.

MARK BATTERSON
NEW YORK TIMES BESTSELLING AUTHOR AND
LEAD PASTOR OF NATIONAL COMMUNITY CHURCH

There are very few people I endorse without reservation. Tony Morgan is on that list. His wisdom and insight is exceptional. Having watched him help more than two hundred churches over the years, I've seen his advice create great benefit to churches looking to get unstuck. Read him, and follow his advice.

WILLIAM VANDERBLOEMEN
FOUNDER AND CEO
VANDERBLOEMEN SEARCH GROUP

Tony offers pragmatic, actionable advice, deeply rooted in experience, any church leader, no matter the size of their church, can use to catalyze the next season of growth. As I read the book, I kept saying, "Yes, that is so true."

GREG L. HAWKINS
AUTHOR OF *MOVE AND MORE*
FORMER EXECUTIVE PASTOR OF
WILLOW CREEK COMMUNITY CHURCH

Tony Morgan has been getting the church unstuck for many years. Now he has brought years of congealed wisdom from helping hundreds of churches into *The Unstuck Church*. The message is simply strong—no church has to get or remain stuck. This book is a huge step in the right direction. Churches and leaders will be reading, learning, getting unstuck, and growing again.

SAM CHAND
LEADERSHIP CONSULTANT AND AUTHOR OF
LEADERSHIP PAIN (WWW.SAMCHAND.COM)

There has never been a more important time for this book. With 80% of churches plateaued or declining and thousands closing their doors annually we all know there has to be a better redemptive alternative. Tony Morgan doesn't just believe it's possible, but he shows us how with proven solutions forged in the real world of church ministry.

GENE APPEL, SENIOR PASTOR
EASTSIDE CHRISTIAN CHURCH
ANAHEIM, CALIFORNIA

When you are on the front lines, you need a practical field manual. And it had better be written by someone who has "been there" and knows what they're talking about. *The Unstuck Church* is a field manual for church leaders in the twenty-first century. And Tony Morgan's strategic gifts, passion for the church, and extensive experience uniquely qualify him to help every church leader. If you are serious about leading a church that is life-giving and life-changing, this book is a must read.

LANCE WITT
FOUNDER, REPLENISH MINISTRIES

The Unstuck Church will challenge you to honestly evaluate where you are on the church life cycle and push you to move forward with a greater focus on the mission of Christ.

JENTEZEN FRANKLIN
SENIOR PASTOR, FREE CHAPEL
NEW YORK TIMES BESTSELLING AUTHOR

Tony Morgan is a highly experienced church leader who understands what it takes to grow a healthy church. His new book, *The Unstuck Church*, is packed with strategic insights about the life cycle of a local church, with a clear path for preventing getting stuck or breaking out of being stuck! Tony will challenge your notions of what church is supposed to be, in order that your church may become all that it can be.

DAN REILAND, EXECUTIVE PASTOR
12STONE CHURCH
LAWRENCEVILLE, GEORGIA

The Unstuck Church is for every church leader who wants their church to grow and keep on growing! Tony Morgan does a brilliant job of defining the stages of growth and decline and shows us how to get "unstuck" and growing again. If your church is stuck, or you don't want to get stuck, this book is for you!

DAVE FERGUSON, LEAD PASTOR
COMMUNITY CHRISTIAN CHURCH
LEAD VISIONARY, NEWTHING
AUTHOR OF *FINDING YOUR WAY BACK TO GOD* AND *STARTING OVER*

NEXT
LEADERSHIP NETWORK

THE UNSTUCK CHURCH

Equipping Churches to
Experience Sustained Health

TONY MORGAN

THOMAS NELSON
Since 1798

Published in Nashville, Tennessee, by Thomas Nelson. Thomas Nelson is a registered trademark of HarperCollins Christian Publishing, Inc.

Thomas Nelson titles may be purchased in bulk for educational, business, fund-raising, or sales promotional use. For information, please e-mail SpecialMarkets@ThomasNelson.com.

Unless otherwise indicated, all Scripture quotations are taken from the *Holy Bible*, New Living Translation. © 1996, 2004, 2007, 2013, 2015 by Tyndale House Foundation. Used by permission of Tyndale House Publishers, Inc., Carol Stream, Illinois 60188. All rights reserved.

Scripture quotations marked (NIV) are taken from the Holy Bible, New International Version®, NIV®. Copyright © 1973, 1978, 1984, 2011 by Biblica, Inc.™ Used by permission of Zondervan. All rights reserved worldwide. www.zondervan.com. The "NIV" and "New International Version" are trademarks registered in the United States Patent and Trademark Office by Biblica, Inc.™

Library of Congress Control Number: 2016954718

ISBN: 978–0718–0944–1–6 (Softcover)
ISBN: 978–0718–0772–6–6 (e-book)

Printed in the United States of America

17 18 19 20 LSC 6 5 4 3 2 1

This book is dedicated to the #UnstuckTeam.
It's a privilege to serve beside you.

ABOUT Leadership✻Network

Leadership Network fosters innovation movements that activate the church to greater impact. We help shape the conversations and practices of pacesetter churches in North America and around the world. The Leadership Network mindset identifies church leaders with forward-thinking ideas—and helps them to catalyze those ideas, resulting in movements that shape the church.

Together with HarperCollins Christian Publishing, the biggest name in Christian books, the NEXT imprint of Leadership Network moves ideas to implementation for leaders to take their ideas to form, substance, and reality. Placed in the hands of other church leaders, that reality begins spreading from one leader to the next . . . and to the next . . . and to the next, where that idea begins to flourish into a full-grown movement that creates a real, tangible impact in the world around it.

NEXT: A LEADERSHIP NETWORK RESOURCE COMMITTED TO HELPING YOU GROW YOUR NEXT IDEA.

LEADNET.ORG/NEXT

CONTENTS

PREFACE

This is going to be your only warning.

I am not a theologian. I've studied Scripture for thirty years, but I know there are countless men and women who have far greater wisdom than I regarding the doctrines of our faith.

I am a Christ follower. I want every person to know the transformation I've experienced. I want as many people as possible to have the forgiveness, love, hope, and purpose that only Jesus can provide.

This book is not designed to revisit the tenets of our faith. There are other disrupters who have done that and continue to do that in our generation.

But I *am* a disrupter. This book is designed to revisit the methods we embrace in the church. (We really do worship our methods.)

I understand this is a risky move. Because my livelihood is based on helping churches get unstuck, there's a chance I may alienate the very people who might hire our team. Because of the urgency I sense to help reach people outside the faith and outside the church, though, I'm willing to embrace that risk.

This book is going to offend you. In one moment, you will feel affirmed because what I have to share will align with your preferences and your ministry approach. Keep reading. Your turn will come. If you don't get to the point where you slam this book shut and lay it aside for a time, then I haven't done my job.

My goal is to challenge your notions of what church is *supposed* to be. I want you to think about the people who need Jesus in their lives. What are you willing to do to reach lost people?

Let's wrestle with what God has designed the church to be. If we engage that journey, my hope is we'll also discover how to get the church unstuck.

TONY MORGAN
LEAD STRATEGIST
THE UNSTUCK GROUP

ACKNOWLEDGMENTS
The Credits

Before anyone sees what I write, my wife, Emily, adds her editorial touch. Thanks, my girl, for partnering with me to get my words out. They really ought to start putting your name on the cover.

Thanks to my teammates at The Unstuck Group for picking up the slack while I was working on this project. I want to specifically acknowledge the contributions of Tiffany Deluccia and Ryan Stigile. Their fingerprints are all over this book.

I'm grateful for leaders like Bill Hybels, Rick Warren, and Andy Stanley, who have changed the way I think about leadership and ministry strategy within the church. What a legacy they're building!

Thanks to Tom Paterson, Pete Richardson, Doug Slaybaugh, and the other voices at the Paterson Center who helped me put legs to our process for helping churches get unstuck.

I'd like to thank LeeEric Fesko and the rest of the team at Thomas Nelson for adding strength to this book from beginning to end. Along those lines, I appreciate the encouragement from Greg Ligon and the crew at the Leadership Network for helping to launch this resource. Thanks for your partnership.

And thank you, Jesus, for letting me serve you and your church. You gave me new life, and now I get to engage your mission. I'm so blessed.

INTRODUCTION
The Life Cycle of Churches

The Unstuck Group has served hundreds of churches and church leaders over the last five years through coaching and consulting engagements. As you might imagine, churches come in all sorts of shapes and sizes. There are various denominations that shape distinct doctrines. There are megachurches and smaller churches. New churches and churches that have been around for decades. Urban, suburban, and rural churches. Churches from a variety of cultures reflecting the diversity of the communities they're trying to reach. Single-location churches and multisite churches. That's just the beginning of the variety we've encountered. Every church is certainly unique.

Yet, regardless of their uniqueness, every church has the potential to go through a very similar life cycle. The life cycle of an organization is usually represented by a bell curve shaped like this one:

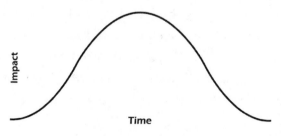

The curve represents how, over time, organizations start, grow, thrive, decline, and eventually end. The horizontal axis represents time, and the vertical axis is an indication of success or impact. In the case of business, that impact might be measured in profit or stock value. This is a picture of the journey from birth to death. People experience this journey, and so do organizations, including churches. In fact, those are the exact terms Aubrey Malphurs uses to describe this journey.

Malphurs first introduced me to this concept through his book *Advanced Strategic Planning: A New Model for Church and Ministry Leaders.* This is one of the bibles for those of us who help churches through consulting and coaching. Malphurs challenges churches to determine where they are on the life cycle curve. In the most recent edition of his book, Malphurs explained it in this way:

> Like people, churches have a life cycle. In general, a church is born and over time it grows. Eventually it reaches a plateau, and if nothing is done to move it off that plateau, it begins to decline. If nothing interrupts the decline, it will die.[1]

The reality is that organizations, including churches, can get stuck in any season of the life cycle. That's why it's important to determine what *season* the organization is in. Then we can intentionally interrupt it. The necessary interruption will look different based on where the church is on its life cycle. Without the interruption, though, the church will remain stuck, and the natural pull will be toward decline and death. Without interruption, death is inevitable. Because of that, I pray God reveals the interruption your church needs to experience its full potential.

The concept of evaluating churches to determine where they are in their life cycle is also included in the strategic planning process developed by Tom Paterson and is known as StratOp. Several years ago, I was trained as a facilitator in this process through the Paterson Center. At The Unstuck Group we use StratOp as a foundational component to help churches get unstuck. StratOp helps organizations clarify where they are through a perspective phase and then develop a strategy that turns planning into action.

Part of the StratOp perspective process includes completing a life cycle analysis. StratOp uses the same bell curve but encourages organizations to determine whether the components of their strategy are accelerating, booming, decelerating, or tanking. Again, the challenge is to determine where they are now. With that information, an organization can begin to put together a plan of action to determine how to move forward in the future—the interruption.

In recent years, my thinking on the life cycle of organizations has been further complemented by Les McKeown's book *Predictable Success: Getting Your Organization on the Growth Track—and Keeping It There*. McKeown, writing more specifically for businesses, uses seven very descriptive terms to highlight seven different stages of an organization.

1. Early Struggle
2. Fun
3. Whitewater
4. Predictable Success
5. Treadmill
6. The Big Rut
7. Death Rattle

What I particularly appreciate about his take is that rather than the pinnacle of the life cycle focusing on plateauing, as with Malphur's version, McKeown challenges organizations to view the top of the life cycle as that stage where "you can set (and consistently achieve) your goals and objectives with a consistent, predictable degree of success."[2]

For business, that success is all about the bottom line—money. Though my mission is to help churches get unstuck, I love the periodic opportunities I have to serve businesses, particularly when the owner is committed to kingdom impact. Businesses are driven by the bottom line. They want to make money. They know that if they don't make money, they will eventually go out of business. If you ask a business owner about the end result of achieving predictable success, I'm guessing at least nine times out of ten you'll hear something about achieving a stronger financial bottom line.

Because they are so committed to the bottom line, I've found these characteristics are true of the businesses I've helped:

- They track the bottom line. Everyone on the team knows whether or not their business is meeting their financial objectives.
- If they aren't making money, there's a sense of urgency that change needs to happen.
- When they do make money, they don't settle. They're always considering "How can we reach more customers and grow the business?"
- They are very focused. If something isn't adding to the bottom line, they stop doing it.

I believe churches have a bottom line as well. Jesus defined it for us after his resurrection. He told his disciples:

I have been given all authority in heaven and on earth. Therefore, go and make disciples of all the nations, baptizing them in the name of the Father and the Son and the Holy Spirit. Teach these new disciples to obey all the commands I have given you. And be sure of this: I am with you always, even to the end of the age. (Matt. 28:18–20)

I can say, unashamedly, that I wish churches were as committed to their bottom line as businesses are to theirs. Unfortunately, I've found these characteristics are true of way too many churches:

- They don't track their bottom line. Most people on the team don't know whether or not the church is meeting its discipleship objectives.
- If they aren't growing (making disciples and baptizing new believers), then many churches don't have a sense of urgency that change needs to happen.
- If there's a sense that what they're doing isn't working, churches tend to settle. They build ministries and programming around the people who are already at the church rather than consider how they can reach more people and grow the kingdom.
- They are rarely focused. If something isn't adding to the bottom line, it doesn't matter. They keep doing it.

Churches have the world's greatest mission; after all, eternity is at stake. I'm convinced we should be doing everything possible short of sin to see lives changed forever. With that, I want churches to strive for the pinnacle of the life cycle, where they are continually making new disciples and experiencing what I refer to as *sustained health*. In other words, I don't want this Matthew 28 season to be a brief moment in time, and I certainly don't want churches stuck someplace short of their potential. I want more churches to arrive at this place of maximum kingdom impact and stay there. I want it to sustain.

Throughout the rest of this book, I will introduce seven phases of a church's life cycle. I've encountered churches in each of these seasons as I've helped them get unstuck. After I describe each phase, I'll offer some specific and strategic next steps—interruptions—that your church can take. I challenge you to determine where your church is on the life cycle, and then, as a team, identify how to move forward with strength and health. For the purposes of furthering this discussion, let's look at the various stages of every church graphically like this:

First, let me provide a quick overview of the life cycle of a typical church, and then we'll take a bit of a deep dive into each specific stage.

Launch

We'll begin with the Launch phase. This is the starting line. In this period, everything is new. There's a new congregation with a new pastor and a new mission. This is a time for dreaming about what the church could potentially be in the future. It's exciting and scary at the same time. The leaders celebrate every time someone shows up, and they, at the same time, regularly wonder if anyone will show up.

Typically these are brand-new churches taking their very first steps, but there are also a small number of churches that choose a fresh start and get to launch all over again. That's a very rare breed. We'll address those unique churches later.

Momentum Growth

The next step is the Momentum Growth phase. This may be the most fun season in the life cycle of a church. During this time, it's as if nothing can go wrong. People start showing up and inviting their friends. New people invite new people. Growth seems to be happening supernaturally.

In this season, the momentum is contagious. It's as if the church leadership can't do anything wrong. Every time the church opens its doors, more new people show up. If this were a business, the mantra would be "make more sales." In the church, though, the focus is clear: reach more people.

Strategic Growth

As the church continues to grow, a tension begins to develop. The church is not able to sustain its growth pace without establishing clear strategies and systems. Some churches then move into the Strategic Growth phase. There's a shift from personalities to teams. The entrepreneurial bent is complemented by an awareness that structure and systems need to be established.

In many cases, this is the first time that churches recognize it's more than getting people to show up; that is, they also have to help people grow through a discipleship path that encourages spiritual formation. If the Momentum Growth phase was about reaching more people, the Strategic Growth phase is about helping people move from where they are to where God wants them to be.

Sustained Health

My prayer is that every church will experience the Sustained Health phase. In this stage, churches embrace the tension between vision and systems. They straddle the fine line between outreach and spiritual formation. Growth continues to occur not only with numbers but also with people accepting Christ, engaging a discipleship process, and sacrificing their lives to get on mission with Jesus.

There are more people showing up *and* there are more people becoming fully devoted to carrying out the Great Commission and the Great Commandment. People embrace their life mission. Not only that, but these ministries become reproducing churches. They start multiplying their impact through church planting and/or engaging a multisite strategy. This is the Acts 1:8 church in action.

Maintenance

I wish every church could stay in the Sustained Health phase, but unfortunately, that's not reality. Some churches slip into the Maintenance phase. I don't think any ministry moves into this season intentionally, but this is the path every church drifts toward if intentional steps aren't taken to avoid it.

What's crazy about this phase is that, on the surface, everything about the church can still appear very healthy. Growth is likely still happening, though at a slower pace. The church may be financially healthier than it has ever been. That said, there will be red flags. The ministries begin to focus more on the people who are already connected to the church than the people they are trying to reach. The focus scale tips toward sustaining systems and structure rather than staying focused on the vision. Methods begin to supersede mission.

Preservation

If churches aren't careful, the next step is the Preservation phase. By the time churches land in this season, it's very difficult to turn things around. In many instances, this is the first time churches begin to experience a decline in both attendance and giving. By now, the methods are sacred. The congregation will run any pastor out of town who attempts to change the worship style or the ministry programming.

In this season, many people grow concerned about the decline of the church, and the commonly perceived solution is to try to reconnect with the people who have left. What the church needs, of course, is fresh leadership and a fresh vision. The challenge is that by the time churches slip into the Preservation phase, the strongest leaders and visionaries have either left of their own volition or they've been forced out.

Life Support

Finally, we get to the Life Support phase. Once a church ends up here, they either close their doors or experience a relaunch. As we'll cover later, I'm surprised at how many churches would choose to die rather than experience a rebirth.

It's that stubborn attachment to the past, though, that leads to the church's ultimate demise. Traditions win over life transformation. Personal preferences crowd out sacrifice and full devotion to the gospel mandate. Attendance dissipates and the money ultimately runs out. I wish it were the fact that people weren't being reached for Jesus that precipitated the urgency that comes with the Life Support phase. Unfortunately, that urgency usually doesn't become pervasive until the money begins to run dry.

As I said, we get to work with all kinds of churches. Every church we've served, though, has landed in one of these stages in the life cycle. We're about ready to unpack every season and highlight the key next steps that are required in each phase along the way. Before we move forward, though, the obvious question is, where is your church in the life cycle?

I'm going to do my best in the following pages to help you discern where your church lands. Are you in the Launch mode? Have you started to experience Momentum Growth? Are you beginning to get intentional about Strategic Growth? Are you currently celebrating a season of Sustained Health? Do you fear that the pinnacle of the church's impact is in the rearview mirror and you've slipped into Maintenance mode? Are the warning signs starting to indicate you've moved into Preservation? Are the remaining church leaders beginning to talk about the end game because the church is on Life Support?

Unfortunately, it's very difficult to make this prognosis on your own. When you're living in the ministry, it's almost impossible to arrive at an unbiased understanding of the church's health. You can't see the forest for the trees. When you know you've been called by God and the mission is clear, it's difficult to assess whether your church is on the upslope or the downslope.

Just to make matters worse, numbers can lie. It's certainly important that we monitor attendance and giving because they offer a barometer of a church's health. As I highlighted above, though, it's very possible for a church to be growing in both attendance and giving but be slipping into Maintenance mode and starting to decline.

I know your tendency at this point will be to jump to the chapter that best reflects where your church is on the life cycle today. I know I would. If you jump ahead, though, I strongly encourage you to read this entire book for a couple of reasons. First, you and your team may read through the various phases of the life cycle and find that your initial gut reaction was wrong. It may be hard to make an accurate assessment until you fully understand the symptoms associated with each phase.

Second, it's going to help you in the future to have a better understanding of all stages of the life cycle. As an example, if your church is on the upslope right now, you will benefit from seeing the symptoms of churches that are in decline. That will help you become more strategic about how you lead going forward to avoid those same symptoms from creeping into your strategy and culture. On the other hand, if your church is in decline today, it will certainly help you to see what churches on the other side of the life cycle are doing to move toward sustained health. The opportunity you have is to launch a whole new life cycle from wherever you are today.

So where is your church? Let's try to bring more clarity to that question and allow you to begin to determine the appropriate interruption. Once that's established, we can help you confirm your next steps as you move toward sustained health.

CHAPTER 1

LAUNCH

Let's Build Something New!

I'm an entrepreneur, so I love this season in the life of a church. If I had believed God called me to preach, I would have planted churches. But I'm not a preacher. Because of that, I'm doing the next best thing. I've launched a ministry to help churches get unstuck. Though I've never launched a church, I've experienced the same emotions and challenges I've heard my church planting friends mention. It seems that launching a business or a nonprofit must be very similar to launching a church.

You start something new and wonder if anyone will buy your service. When you're the business owner (or church planter), you're constantly feeling the tension of wanting to fulfill the new mission of the organization, while at the same time you're wondering if there will be enough money to provide for the people on your team. More important, you ponder if there will be enough money to put food on *your* table.

The resource challenge is real. I've heard many stories from church planters in those early days. The dreams for the future drive the passion to succeed. There's a real sense of calling and mission. At the same time, this season tests the faith of the most prayerful church planter. It's a week-to-week journey, wondering who will show up and how much people will give. Because of that, many churches in this launch season live from one offering to the next. It's like living paycheck to paycheck.

What I love about these churches, though, is that the mission is clear. Regardless of theology or methodology, the churches that survive and move on to the next season of growth have one thing in common: they want to reach more people for Jesus. That approach, of course, looks different for different churches, but it's that focus of reaching new people that unifies (or in some cases repels) people who connect to these new ministries.

You should know that a clear mission for why the church exists will certainly repel some people. I remember Mark Beeson, the founding and senior pastor of Granger Community Church in Granger, Indiana, talking about the well-intentioned people who tried to give organs to the church in their early days. Mark had no intention of using organ music. It didn't fit into their clear mission of helping people take their next steps toward Christ together.

Granger's mission was very clear, and so was Mark's approach for how the church would accomplish that mission. Because of that, hundreds of people visited the church in those early days, and some people even started giving. I remember Mark explaining years later, though, that not everyone stayed. In fact, Granger lost their top giver in each of the first three years. It's just one example of how the financial resource challenge is very evident in this launch season of most churches.

Fortunately, as we'll see later, there are churches, networks, and denominations that recognize these financial challenges and help to begin to reproduce new ministries through church planting and multisite strategy. Without that support, the church must scrape to get by until it gets to a place of critical mass where the church can financially sustain its mission.

It's encouraging, though, to hear the stories (the miracles) of how God provides. Someone anonymously sends a check for thousands of dollars that arrives out of the blue. A new family with a conviction for generosity shows up at just the right time to begin financially supporting the ministry. God provides just the right building at just the right price for the church to hold worship services. Every successful church launch experiences these miracles. It's a great reminder that it's the Lord who is building his church.

Speaking of worship services, that's really the focus for just about every new church launch. Churches may begin with a home group, one-on-one relationships, or a local outreach effort to begin connecting with people. But ultimately there really needs to be a gathering for the church to experience momentum growth.

Those gatherings, of course, will look different from church to church, but there's something powerful that happens when people come together to worship, learn, and connect with others. People leave encouraged to take their next steps, and the church becomes unified to accomplish its mission.

With that said, let me recap some of the characteristics of churches in this launch season:

1. *It's a new beginning.* There's a fresh purpose for what the church will accomplish. The leadership, particularly the pastor, has big dreams for the future.
2. *There's a priority on reaching new people.* Part of this is

because it's a reflection of why the church exists, and part of it is out of the necessity to reach critical mass so the church can survive.

3. *There's a heavy reliance on volunteer engagement.* Because the church is new and financial resources are limited, the pastor will welcome anyone who's willing to help.

4. *Very little competes with weekend worship services.* Most of the attention and volunteer engagement is centered around the teaching, worship, children's ministry, and guest environments.

5. *There are few, if any, rules.* The pastor is typically involved in every decision. Rules or systems are really not needed at this point. It's all about executing the pastor's direction.

6. *Finances are tight.* New people don't give. People are, without a doubt, consumers before they are contributors. That happens with people's time and certainly their money.

Ed Stetzer worked with the North American Mission Board and surveyed two thousand church plants. Through his research, he determined that one-third of churches fail within the first four years.[1] My desire, though, isn't for a church just to survive; I want to see churches thrive and move into the next season of momentum growth.

For churches in the launch phase, your goal is pretty simple: you need to get through the birthing process as soon as possible. With that in mind, let's review some of the key steps required to move forward.

Start with Strong Leadership: You Need a Leader More than You Need a Pastor or Preacher

Though someone will likely have the title of pastor, churches that move from launch to momentum must have strong leadership, and that begins with the church planter. In fact, if pushed to prioritize what these new churches need most, I would select a leader, then a preacher (a capable teacher), and then a pastor (the caring shepherd), in that order.

Leadership is a gift. It's among the spiritual gifts listed in Scripture: "If God has given you leadership ability, take the responsibility seriously" (Rom. 12:8). A couple of verses earlier, though, the Bible also says, "God has given us different gifts for doing certain things well" (v. 6). This implies that some people have leadership abilities and others do not. Though we are all followers, not all of us are leaders. Anyone can learn leadership skills, but not everyone is gifted to be a leader.

God has also designed the church to have clear leadership roles and structures. For example, the Bible mentions "the gifts Christ gave to the church: the apostles, the prophets, the evangelists, and the pastors and teachers" (Eph. 4:11). These are specific roles God designed for ministry.

I've worked with many churches in which the senior pastor is a great shepherd. His primary giftedness is around loving and caring for people. He has a pastoral strength that is crucial when people are hurting. This is an important gift within the body of Christ, but it's not the primary gift I'd want in the senior pastor leading a church through the birthing process if the goal is more than just survival.

I've also worked with many churches that have senior pastors who are extremely gifted teachers and preachers. Communicating the truth of Scripture is a critical component of a healthy church. After all: "How can they call on him to save them unless they believe in him? And how can they believe in him if they have never heard about him? And how can they hear about him unless someone tells them?" (Rom. 10:14). The challenge is that I've seen many dead and declining churches led by pastors with great wisdom who were very capable preachers. But they couldn't lead.

In each of these instances, what was missing was leadership. One of the common characteristics of declining churches is that they lack strong leadership. Though any healthy church will need scores of gifted leaders in both staff and lay leadership roles, in no role is this more important than that of the senior pastor. It may not be that person's primary spiritual gift, but it must be in the mix of core strengths pastors bring to their role.

There are some people in leadership positions who aren't really leaders. Leaders aren't leaders just because they have a title. I'm not talking about positional leadership. Instead, I'm talking about the leadership required to move the church forward from where it is to where God wants it to be.

When there is uncertainty for the future, real leaders clarify the vision for where the organization is going.

When a good opportunity pops up that pulls the organization from its core mission, real leaders say no.

When ministries are pulling in different directions, real leaders prioritize what's important now.

When conflicts arise around competing core values, real leaders lead through the conflict to preserve unity.

When they make mistakes, real leaders are quick to admit responsibility and learn from those mistakes.

When mistakes are made by someone else, real leaders are quick to take responsibility and help others learn from those mistakes.

When the team gets comfortable and content to stick with past practices, real leaders challenge the status quo.

When there is work to be completed and deadlines to make, real leaders will still prioritize time for leadership development and equipping others.

When talented, high-capacity people join the team, real leaders let others lead, but they never give away accountability.

When someone continually drops the ball, real leaders step in to coach and redirect.

When someone continually ignores the coaching, real leaders remove people from the team.

When consensus is impossible and people are watching, real leaders make decisions and know criticism will follow.

When the future is set and a team has clear vision, values, and priorities, real leaders empower others to make decisions.

When crisis hits and people are searching for direction, real leaders proceed quickly and decisively.

With all of that being said, though, do you know the biggest challenge of being a leader? It's this: eventually real leaders have to get out in front and actually lead. Only strong, gifted leaders are willing to do that.

Let me add one additional side note before we move on. I previously highlighted the priority of the senior pastor as being a leader, then a preacher, and then a pastor, in that order. Ironically, churches on the opposite end of the life cycle—those in the preservation and life support phases—routinely reverse this order. These declining churches first look to hire a pastor, then a preacher, and then a leader. That's one of the primary reasons they are where they are on the life cycle.

Identify Who You Are Trying to Reach: You Need to Identify Your Target Audience (and It Needs to Be Younger)

When The Unstuck Group helps churches through a strategic planning process, one of the exercises we facilitate has to do with confirming the "primary customer" the church is trying to reach.

What we've learned, of course, is that when a church tries to reach *everyone*, they rarely connect with anyone effectively. On the other hand, when they focus on who they are trying to reach, they can get very intentional and effective in reaching that person. Ironically, they oftentimes reach all kinds of people in the process.

This is one area where I believe the church in America falls short. We don't really know the people we are trying to reach.

If we were missionaries in another country, we would purposely get to know the language and the customs to more effectively accomplish our mission. In our communities, though, we jump straight to our mission while ignoring the language and customs of the people we're trying to reach.

I've led a couple of churches through a planning process in which they identified one of their key customers as a professional in their community. For them, it wasn't necessarily a matter of gender, age, or ethnicity. That's not unusual. The customer in most communities these days is not likely going to be a specific race or gender. In fact, diversity is attractive to more and more people. What these churches identified was a target mind-set.

Based on the communities where the churches were situated, they determined their mission fields are primarily made up of professionals.

During that experience, Glenn Llopis's article "The Content You Read Shapes How You Lead" caught my eye.[2] His team's study determined the top ten content themes that leaders consume. In other words, they're learning the language of their audience.

Many of the top themes they identified are key themes we find in the Bible. If you're a church leader trying to connect with professionals, you should find this very encouraging and do what you can to learn from their approach. Here are some examples of the themes they identified:

- **"Managing People":** Llopis wrote, "Leaders hunger to understand human behavior so they can inspire and motivate people to reach their full potential." Isn't that what discipleship is all about? What would it look like to tap that desire to help others? People want to know that their lives count, and how they influence others is a key component.
- **"Change Management":** Llopis observed, "Leaders want to feel more comfortable and capable leading in times of crisis and uncertainty." We will all face crisis and uncertainty. Wouldn't it be incredible if we equipped people for those circumstances when they're facing crisis themselves or with a friend?
- **"Make More Money":** Remember, we need to understand the people we are trying to reach. If they're trying to make more money, we should embrace that and look for opportunities to share what Scripture has to say on

that. Don't be afraid to teach on money. The people we're trying to reach are looking for answers.

- **"Relationships"**: As we know, God designed us for relationships. There are too many "one anothers" in the Bible for us not to help people engage new disciplines to build and sustain healthy relationships. If anyone should be the thought leader on this topic, it should be the church.

- **"Time Management"**: Llopis offered, "Leaders want to get the most out of every day and seek to find new ways to manage their time in order to influence growth, innovation and opportunity." People are busy. They need help prioritizing their lives. Don't you want to help people consider how they can be better stewards of not only their money but their time?

The list could go on, but you get the point. We need to know who we are trying to reach. That goes beyond demographics; we also need to know their mind-set. Once we understand that, we can better connect with their needs and help them take their next steps toward Christ.

This principle is particularly important for new churches. Remember, the underlying motivation at this point is that we're trying to get through the launch phase as soon as possible. Because of that, the temptation will be to try to be all things to all people. Just the opposite is true. To be effective in building a crowd, you need to know specifically who you are trying to reach.

Churches hate this conversation, because we really do want to reach *all* people. That's a righteous desire because it reflects God's heart as well. He "wants everyone to be saved and to understand the truth" (1 Tim. 2:4). The problem, of course, is, if you try to be all things to all people, you become very ineffective at reaching anyone. Newer, smaller churches don't have the people, resources, and time to reach every person of every nation. Instead, we have to begin in our Jerusalem (Acts 1:8).

The fact is that every church, whether they want to believe it or not, has a target customer. And most times, age is a big distinguishing factor. In fact, it may still be *the* distinguishing factor. Generally, when I walk into a church, it doesn't take very long to determine if the church is targeting young adults (under thirty-five), middle-aged adults (thirty-five to fifty-four), or older adults (over fifty-four).

Your target audience may not be written down on paper, but everything the church does and communicates will point to one of these key target audiences. The question is, are you targeting the right age group?

With that, let me share some research I discovered from Nielsen. They completed a study of consumers and their responses to online advertising campaigns. They reviewed nearly five thousand campaigns in the process. Here's what they found:

> A look at specific age breaks indicate that ad campaigns geared towards the 21–34 age range were able to reach consumers 62 percent of the time. Meanwhile, campaigns targeting consumers aged 35–54, reach their audiences just 41 percent of the time. This is despite the fact that those 21–34 represent only 22 percent of the online population, compared with one-third for consumers 35–54.[3]

Now, there are a lot of numbers in that paragraph, so it may be easy to miss the point. The bottom line is this: if you target young adults, you will reach more of the total audience than if you target middle-aged adults (boomers and Gen Xers).

Let me put this into practical terms:

- If your music, environments, ministries, and other programming make older adults happy (my parents), you're reaching older adults.
- If your music, environments, ministries, and other programming make middle-aged adults happy (me), you will reach middle-aged adults *and* many older adults.
- If your music, environments, ministries, and other programming make young adults happy (my kids), you will reach young adults *and* many middle-aged *and* older adults.

That's why advertisers target young adults with their ad campaigns. That's why television stations target young adults with their programming. That's why musicians target young adults with their music.

Here's a little secret: Older adults want to be younger. Middle-aged adults want to be younger. Young adults don't want to be older. It's not about age; it's about their mind-set.

Now let's go back to my original question. Do you know your customer? Who are you trying to reach? Take a look at everything you are doing and saying. Does it reflect that audience?

Let me tell you the story of Cowboy Junction Church in Hobbs, New Mexico. As the name of the church suggests, they have a unique customer. They're trying to reach people in their community who live the western lifestyle. No, not everyone is a cowboy, but they do have cowboys in their congregation. In fact, they've been trying to reach cowboys from the very beginning of the church.

Because reaching cowboys and other people with that western mind-set was their primary focus, the church started by holding services on Monday evening rather than Sunday morning. That's a strategy I'm guessing church planting networks would never recommend, but it made complete sense for Cowboy Junction Church. In the early days, most of the people who the church was reaching were participating in rodeos on the weekends. On Sunday mornings, the church's congregation was calf roping, bull riding, and barrel racing.

The church could have held services on Sundays, but they would have completely missed the primary demographic they were trying to reach. Cowboy Junction Church recognized their ministry strategy shouldn't mimic what other churches were doing. Instead, their ministry strategy needed to reflect the people they were trying to reach, even if that meant holding worship services on Monday evening.

Here's the reality. People inside the church can get very loud. Those voices are much louder than the people outside the church. That's why churches focus inward. They let their inside voices drive everything. As soon as you make that shift and begin to prioritize the inside voices, your church is guaranteed to decline. We'll hit that much harder later on.

Let me state the obvious here: it's a lot easier for a church to focus what they do around a specific target audience when the church is in the launch phase. The further you get through the life cycle, the harder it gets to identify and refocus ministry, including worship services, around a specific mind-set. My encouragement for the churches who are in these early stages is to make the tough calls now, because it won't get any easier. But it will always be necessary if you hope to reach people for Jesus.

Determine the Primary Purpose of Your Ministry: You Need a Mission That Turns Some People Away from Your Church

One of the first things any leader of a new organization must do is establish the primary purpose for why the organization exists. We call this a mission statement. This really is foundational not only to the early days of a church but also to focus the church on its core purpose in the years to come.

Let's not confuse the mission with your vision statement. I believe you need both. The mission statement is a concise phrase, mantra, or slogan that captures the heartbeat of what your church is all about. The vision statement, on the other hand, describes where you picture the church to be heading in the future. We'll talk more about that later.

When crafting a mission statement, I'm a big fan of the "less is more" philosophy. I encourage churches to stick with a phrase that's twelve words or less. You want it to be easy for everyone to remember. The statement should express to your congregation, your staff, your volunteers, and your community what your church is all about.

As I mentioned earlier, one of the churches The Unstuck Group has served is Cowboy Junction Church. Their mission statement is pretty straightforward:

Love God. Love people. No limits.

I love that! It succinctly captures why the church exists and includes a bit of their cowboy attitude as well. There are no limits to how they'll love God and people.

North Point Community Church in Atlanta has a similarly concise statement. They say it this way:

> WE LEAD PEOPLE INTO A GROWING
> RELATIONSHIP WITH JESUS CHRIST.

Nothing flashy. Very straightforward. That statement explains all that the church is about. Although they have other statements to express their vision, strategy, and beliefs, that simple mission statement is the foundation for everything else.

Here's the great thing about having a very clear mission statement that defines why the church exists: it makes it clear whether people should *join* your mission or not. That's a good thing. Hopefully many, many people will be captivated by your mission statement and want to join you and add their gifts and abilities, their time, their prayer support, their money, and so on. Your statement should say, "This is who we are. Do you want to join us on this big mission?"

When you land on a clear statement, it will become the rallying cry that encourages people to take the next step in engaging in what you do. It will be the phrase that everyone remembers and will begin to define who you are and who you are not.

That "who you are not" part is pretty important too. It's especially critical during the launch phase of a church. You are going to meet people with all kinds of backgrounds and experiences as they walk into your church. The hope is that many of them will be eternally impacted by your church's influence in their lives. If you are a healthy church, though, your church won't be for everyone.

Because people have different faith and church experiences in their backgrounds, they have different expectations of what the church should and shouldn't be. That's okay. As I've heard Rick Warren say, "There are all kinds of churches for all kinds of people." You have to decide what kind of church you are going to be. Then you need to be that.

Now, as I mentioned previously, this presents a challenge for a new church. If the church is going to survive and grow, you need several key ingredients, including people and money. I don't care how noble your mission is, if you don't have people and financial resources, your mission will eventually die. If you don't believe me, talk with a church on the other end of the life cycle. They'll help you understand how it takes people and money for a church to stay alive.

With that in mind, I guarantee you will, at some point, have this experience. You will meet a new person at your church. It'll be exciting because you are hoping to connect new people to your mission. What will make this doubly exciting is that you will find out this person has a job. They make money for a living. They have a bank account. Since they have money, there's a chance they might give some of it to your church.

Here's the problem. They're just checking out the church. They like what they've experienced, and they're interested in learning more about how they might get plugged in, but they have some questions they'd like you to answer first. (As a side note, this is one reason why growing churches need to have an easy first experience for new people who are wanting to learn more about the ministry and consider their next steps to connect. It becomes impractical to answer everyone's questions through lengthy one-on-one conversations.)

However, when you hear what they have to say, you realize there's a disconnect. It could be something in their theology. It could be something about their expectations for the worship services. It could be something about your discipleship path. It could be that they are looking for a ministry program you have no intention of ever offering at your church. Whatever the case, you will be at a pivotal point in the life of your ministry.

It's in that moment you will have to decide *if you are really about the mission God has called this church to.* The temptation will certainly be there to bend "this one time" to keep this person and their family. With the financial stress of a new ministry, it will be challenging not to waver just a little on the mission you've established. Are you going to be willing to stick to that mission if a new person tries to pull you down a different path?

These aren't easy decisions. They're the types of decisions, though, that great leaders make when they're faced with something that would force them to compromise. Don't compromise. Don't choose the easy path that many other churches have chosen and attempt to be all things to all people. If you do that, you will never build something great.

Establish a Financial Plan: Hope and Prayer Won't Pay the Bills

I love the Bible. I particularly like the Bible passages that are filled with sarcasm and humor. I believe sarcasm is a spiritual gift. If it wasn't, why would there be passages like this in Scripture:

But don't begin until you count the cost. For who would begin construction of a building without first calculating the cost to see if there is enough money to finish it? Otherwise, you might complete only the foundation before running out of money, and then everyone would laugh at you. They would say, "There's the person who started that building and couldn't afford to finish it!" (Luke 14:28–30)

I use that passage a lot when I'm talking with churches about the importance of planning. Planning is a stewardship discipline. If we don't plan, we run the risk of wasting resources on initiatives that might not be God's priority for the church.

The message of this passage is even more compelling, though, for the churches in the launch phase. Don't launch a church before you count the cost. Seriously. Who would begin launching a church without first figuring out the cost to see if there's enough money to finish it?

Because of that, I want you to imagine three buckets of money.

ONE-TIME
START-UP
COSTS

ONGOING
COSTS
SUPPORTED
BY GIVING

INITIAL GAP
SUPPORTED
BY OUTSIDE
SOURCES

The first bucket is for all the money needed to cover one-time startup costs. It's going to be different for different churches, but that might include rent, audio and video equipment, children's ministry equipment, facility renovations, and so on. Obviously, you need to have funding in place before you launch to cover these one-time expenses.

The second bucket is for the money that will come through giving. You need to have a plan for that money. You know why? Because there's not going to be much of it in the early days. New people, especially people who are coming from outside the church and outside the faith, very likely won't be giving when they show up. You obviously want to minister to those people, but don't expect them to financially contribute right away.

Because of that, you need to have a budget in place to plan how you are going to spend the limited financial resources you will have available. Make a plan before you launch, and modify it based on your actual giving experience. I encourage you to heed this advice: always plan to spend less than you plan to receive in any of your buckets. That buffer will relieve a lot of stress in the long run and free up dollars to follow God's leading.

The third bucket is for the gap between what comes in through your church's giving and what is legitimately required to sustain the ministry through the launch process. It would be highly unusual for a church to be self-sustaining from day one. In fact, it may take several years for a church to stand on its own financially. With that being the case, part of your fund-raising before and after the church is planted must be for this third bucket.

Now, if you're smart, you've already recognized that two of these buckets don't involve people at your church. That may mean you have to consider several other options:

- **You may have to be bivocational for a season.** That's far from ideal, but I did that while my business was launching. I worked two jobs for about three years. Then I had to take a leap and walk away from a regular paycheck because the ministry I was launching needed my full-time attention and I was finally in a position to support our family.

- **You may need to save more before you launch.** This assumes you are out of debt. Debt, without question, limits our ability to say yes to the callings Jesus has for our lives.
- **You may need to have the staff raise their own support.** There are ministries all over the globe that use this strategy to fund their mission. It means sacrificing time and energy to raise support, though, so don't make it a long-term solution.
- **You may have to ask other churches, denominations, or church planting networks for help.** Here's the great news: as more churches move into sustained health in the life cycle, there will be more opportunities to invest in new church launches.

Whatever strategy you use, don't launch with debt. There may be a place at some point in the future to use debt to fund capital needs. But you don't want to go into debt to fund general ministry expenses.

Now, let me talk a bit about bucket number two. You actually get to control not only the money that's going out of that bucket but the money that's coming in as well. Starting with day one, you need to teach what the Bible has to say about money.

I'd begin by letting people know God and his church don't want their money. God wants their hearts. What's interesting, though, is that Jesus said, "Wherever your treasure is, there the desires of your heart will also be" (Matt. 6:21).

If I were Jesus, I would have reversed that statement. I would have said, "Wherever the desire of your heart is, there your treasure will also be." In other words, when God has your heart, he'll also be in control of how you use your money. Jesus taught just the opposite. When we fully trust God with our money, our heart for God follows. People need to hear that.

Churches that are going to get through the launch season and move into the next phase of the life cycle must have a plan to fund the mission. For the church to become self-sustaining, you have to begin establishing this foundation from the very beginning.

Here are some thoughts to consider:

- **People have money problems.** If you don't state the obvious, they're going to assume you're completely disconnected from reality. If this is a challenge people are facing in their personal lives, why not teach what the Bible has to say on that issue?
- **Encourage everyone to participate.** From the very beginning, this needs to apply to everyone. The widow's offering of two small coins is important to the health of the church, but it's more important to the faith journey of the widow.
- **Give people a chance to share their story.** There's going to be a lot of heart change when people begin to give God control of their finances.
- **Encourage people to volunteer.** Serving creates ownership in the mission. Our research shows that people who volunteer also give more to the mission. More on this topic in a moment.
- **Be intentional with your offering times.** Take a few minutes during every service to tie giving to a truth

found in Scripture, a story of life change, or a connection to the church's mission and vision. People need to know they are part of a cause much bigger than themselves.

Let me be blunt. Hope will not pay the bills (though I want you to have hope). Prayer will not pay your salary (though you should certainly pray for God's provision). You need to do what the Bible says you should do. You need to count the cost, and you need to plan before you build.

Give Ministry Away to Volunteers: God Did Not Design the Church for the Pastor to Make Every Hospital Visit

In small churches, the senior pastor is expected to do all the ministry. Unfortunately, if you let this mind-set take hold, you'll end up with one of two results. In one instance, the church will get stuck. Growth will stop because there's only so much ministry one person can do. As you are probably aware, there are thousands of churches across the country that will never grow beyond a hundred people because the senior pastor is doing all the ministry.

In the second instance, the church might grow because it has the financial resources to hire more staff to do the ministry. This only delays and exasperates the challenges the church will ultimately experience. At some point, the church will run out of money to hire more staff. When that happens, it will be very difficult to shift the culture and encourage the people to volunteer in ministry. The expectation will be ingrained in the church that the paid pastors are the ones who do ministry.

For a church hoping to move from the launch phase into

momentum growth, this should be alarming. Why? My experience confirms that churches that empower volunteers to do ministry are healthier than those that don't. When people volunteer, they're more likely to show up for worship. They're also more likely to invite their friends. They give more. Maybe most important, people who engage in ministry will be stretched in their faith. Ministry shapes a person's spiritual formation.

If you are a leader in a church that is in the launch season, though, I know your wiring. You are driven. You want things to get done, and you want them done well. There's something in you that's always saying, "I can do it better."

Pride makes us do stupid things. One of the consequences is falling into the "I can do it better" trap. It's what happens when we look at a situation or a decision and say to ourselves, "I can't let anyone else have this one, because it'll just be easier (and better) if I do it myself."

If you are a perfectionist, people won't like to be around you. It's one thing to give our best effort. It's another thing to think it always has to be perfect. Perfectionism isn't attractive.

Needing to be in control will kill you. It leads to anxiety and fear. It's an indication that God's not in control. It will paralyze you.

If you always do it, no one else will learn to do it, and you will always be stuck thinking you have to do it. It's a vicious cycle.

If you always do it, you're denying other people the opportunity to live out God's purpose for their lives. That's kind of like telling people you know better than God what's best for their lives.

What if Jesus said, "I can do this better." Because, if you think about it, he *could* do it better, but he still elected to give ministry away to others.

When we choose to do it ourselves, we're taking the easy way out. It's harder to find people, train them, coach them, and check up on them. In other words, we're basically admitting we'd rather not do the hard work that could ultimately lead to better results.

The crazy thing about this mind-set is that it directly conflicts with our ministry calling. Remember . . .

> [My] responsibility is to equip God's people to do his work and build up the church, the body of Christ. This will continue until we all come to such unity in our faith and knowledge of God's Son that we will be mature in the Lord, measuring up to the full and complete standard of Christ. (Eph. 4:12–13)

With that direction from Scripture, there's really no room for "I can do it better." In order for me to do what God is calling me to do, I have to equip God's people to do his work. *They* can do it better.

One church that has practiced this since their days in launch mode is Freedom Church in Acworth, Georgia. Of all the churches The Unstuck Group has worked with through the years, Freedom Church has one of the lowest staffing ratios. In other words, they have far fewer staff members when compared to attendance than almost all the churches we have served. One of the reasons they can afford to have so few staff is because they've done so well in mobilizing volunteers.

Todd Lollis, the church's operations pastor, explained their volunteer strategy:

> We want people to understand that our goal is not to recruit people to our ministry but to empower them for theirs. The job of the church staff is not to do the work of the ministry but to

equip others for the work of the ministry. If we are doing our job correctly, we should be able to lead with a lean staff.[4]

You are probably familiar with the story of the early church in Acts 6. That was a church in the launch phase. They were facing the very challenges I'm describing here. The apostles were doing all the ministry themselves, including food distribution to widows. The system was broken. They didn't have time for prayer and teaching. And they said, "We apostles should spend our time teaching the word of God, not running a food program" (Acts 6:2).

I've been in that board meeting before, and likely so have you. God didn't design the pastor to do all the ministry. That's God's design for the body of Christ. This story should alarm you because it suggests *it's possible to do the work of God without doing the work God has called you to do.*

God did not design the church for the pastor to make every hospital visit.

God did not design the church for the pastor to lead every person in a prayer to accept Christ.

God did not design the church for the pastor to be at every wedding and funeral.

God did not design the church for the pastor to be involved in counseling every hurting person.

God did not design the church for the pastor to be the only person who can teach God's Word.

Getting back to our story, the apostles decided they needed to give ministry away. They found seven other leaders to take responsibility for the food distribution. When that happened, the apostles were able to get their focus back to prayer and teaching. As a result of that, "God's message continued to spread. The number of believers greatly increased in Jerusalem, and many of the Jewish priests were converted, too" (Acts 6:7). The church got healthier and started to have a bigger impact!

Let me be blunt again. If you're doing all the ministry, you're probably going to lead an unhealthy, ineffective ministry that's not consistent with God's plan for your life. You have to be willing to give ministry away, and that needs to be one of the overriding characteristics of your church's culture if you want to experience growth and ultimately sustained health.

If you're an entrepreneur like me, the launch phase is an exhilarating season. To summarize, we hit some key strategies during this phase around becoming a strong leader, identifying your primary customer, establishing a mission focus, building a financial plan, and empowering volunteers. Now that we've covered some of the key strategies healthy churches prioritize during the launch phase, it's time to take a step forward on the life cycle. We're going to move from launch to momentum growth.

CHAPTER 2

MOMENTUM GROWTH
It's Going to Be a Wild Ride!

After moving through the launch season, my prayer is that you'll have the opportunity to experience a season of momentum growth. Enjoy this time. In the future, these will be remembered as the glory days of the church. It'll be that season when, almost without explanation, the church made a dramatic leap forward.

A good example of this happened at Heartland Church in Indianapolis. Darryn Scheske planted the church with his wife, Lorree, in 2001. They started with seventeen people in the Scheskes' living room. In that first year, they baptized eighty-eight people and grew to three hundred people in worship attendance. Less than four years later, they had doubled to more than six hundred people. Today the church is reaching more than twenty-three hundred people every weekend.

That's momentum growth. No, it's not at all typical for churches to double in size in such a short period of time. But if you are diligent and faithful in the launch phase of ministry, I believe it's possible to experience rapid growth. I routinely hear stories similar to that of Heartland that mimic the experience of the early church. There are many examples of churches where growth is happening because "each day the Lord added to their fellowship those who were being saved" (Acts 2:47).

I've been through these seasons as a pastor with two different churches. I'm not going to lie. It's exhilarating! Every time the church opens its doors, more people show up. There's new person after new person. There's salvation after salvation. There's baptism after baptism. People visit one week and invite their families and friends to join them the next week. In that moment, you really believe you are part of a revival. You know why? Because it's a revival!

The Lord is building his church! There's a movement happening. People's lives are being transformed in a miraculous way. I remember Bill Hybels, the pastor of Willow Creek Community Church in South Barrington, Illinois, saying, "It's a God thing!" God is alive! Let's celebrate that.

We should continue to pray for revival in the church, but we need to realize there are churches that are experiencing it today. It's actually happening. Rather than trying to explain (or complain) it away by naming everything these churches are doing wrong, maybe it's time to learn from these churches. Maybe we need to imitate their strategy. And maybe we need to pray that Jesus will allow our churches to experience that same revival.

I've been there on Sunday mornings when every seat in the sanctuary was filled. Then every seat in the overflow area filled. Then we started turning people away and encouraging them to come to the next service. God is doing that in churches today.

I've been in the meetings after our worship services have been completely full and we're wrestling with the decision to add another service, add another venue, or open another campus. In this momentum growth season, the conversations are typically a reaction to what's happening. In the next phase of the life cycle, those conversations will become more proactive. Whatever the case, these are the problems *every* church leader wants to have. Growth problems are a lot more fun than decline problems.

You know, there's a story from the early days of the church when Peter was preaching a message to thousands. At the conclusion of his message, he challenged everyone with this word: "Each of you must repent of your sins and turn to God, and be baptized in the name of Jesus Christ for the forgiveness of your sins. Then you will receive the gift of the Holy Spirit" (Acts 2:38). Three thousand people were baptized that day!

Do you believe God is big enough and powerful enough to do that same miracle today? I do. I say that because I've actually been in the water and watched hundreds of people come forward to be baptized and proclaim their faith in Jesus. God is still moving. He is still in the miracle business. He still wants *everyone* to be saved and to know the truth.

Momentum growth looks different in different churches. This season of the life cycle isn't limited to megachurches. As an example, I mentioned our work with Cowboy Junction Church. They're situated in Hobbs, New Mexico, which is nothing like Los Angeles or Dallas or Atlanta. In the last couple of years, they've grown from 375 to 500 people. More amazingly, though, 190 people have accepted Christ through their ministry in the last twelve months. That is momentum growth!

I also mentioned Freedom Church in Acworth, Georgia. The first time we helped them respond to their growth challenges, they were running about seven hundred people in attendance. Their attendance had increased by more than 30 percent the previous year, and they needed help in getting the right people in the right roles. After that process, the church almost doubled in size. We had to revisit their staffing and structure all over again. They're a completely different church than they were a couple of years ago. They've experienced momentum!

Here are some of the characteristics of churches in the momentum growth season:

1. *There's an outward focus.* These churches are unashamed about their desire to reach more people for Jesus. Year after year the numbers are up and to the right. They'll remove whatever barriers they need to continue to connect with people outside the church and outside the faith.

2. *There's a lot of buzz.* The church becomes known in the community. They really don't have to do much external marketing, because word-of-mouth marketing is the primary way people find out about the church. New people invite new people.

3. *Creativity and innovation (and therefore change) are expected.* These churches are risk-driven. I've heard Craig Groeschel from Life.Church say, "We'll do anything short of sin to reach people who don't know Christ." That's the attitude that helps drive innovation in these churches.

4. *They begin to focus their vision.* They mark out the specifics of where their ministries are heading in the future. There's focus of purpose and a focus on the new mountain the ministry team intends to take on.

5. *They are often driven by personality.* For good or bad, the senior pastor is often the single face of the ministry. People know the church because they know the pastor. Part of what distinguishes churches that take the next

step into strategic growth is they multiply the voices and personalities that carry out the ministry strategy.

6. *They begin to give leadership away.* As a result of growth, these churches recognize that one person can't call all the shots. In the launch phase, churches start to give ministry away. In momentum growth, churches start to give leadership away.

When churches hit the momentum growth season, they really need to hold on for the ride. This is an exciting era in the life of any church. Grow, grow, grow. Even if I tried to coach churches to prepare for the next season in the life cycle (strategic growth), they'd probably ignore me. Why should they listen? Everything they're doing is working.

The time will come, though, when the church will outgrow its infrastructure. The complexity created by the number of people connected to the ministry will force the leadership to wrestle with the new challenges of strategic growth. For those willing to listen, though, let's begin to review some of the key next steps required to move forward during this momentum growth phase.

Make Space for Growth: Always Build a New Service Before You Build a New Building

During this season of momentum growth, having adequate space will become a constant pressure. The hardest (and yet easiest) solution will always be to find or build a bigger building. My prayer is that, at some point, you will have to pull that trigger. Before you ever make that move, though, the best step for you is to ask, "Can we add another service?"

Adding services is one of the best strategies you can engage to improve the health of your church. It forces you to multiply the number of leaders in your church. It challenges you to increase the number of volunteers. Both of those shifts will encourage people to embrace more ownership in the ministry. That will make the church healthier, but it will also encourage people to take new steps in their faith journeys as well.

Adding services will challenge you to create new systems to simplify how people connect to the church, how you communicate priority information, how you scale ministry programming, and how you encourage more people to take steps in spiritual formation. All of that makes the church healthier because you are preparing for the next season in your life cycle, which will allow you to become a reproducing church.

Adding services also creates more options for people to check out your church. Consumers like options. The people you are trying to reach will always be consumers before they become committed followers of Christ. More services mean more options, which mean more people hearing the gospel message.

For these reasons and more, I'd much rather a church add more services than find or build a bigger building. I hope you never have the goal to get everyone in your church to attend one service at the same time. Churches that focus inward are more concerned about knowing and seeing every person in the congregation. That's why they invest exorbitant amounts of money to build larger sanctuaries that will accommodate the entire church on Easter Sunday. The higher value, however, should be to reach new people. New people want more options. They don't need a bigger sanctuary.

That said, here's a checklist to help you work through some of the key decision factors to consider as you're evaluating whether or not to add new services.

- **Get to critical mass.** This is going to depend largely on the seating capacity of your sanctuary or auditorium. In many instances, at least half the seats need to be filled for the room to have energy and engagement. If you have less than that, people wonder, *Why aren't people showing up?* Reduce the number of services, remove seats, or use pipe and drape to shrink the room if you don't have critical mass.
- **When you are consistently more than 80 percent full in all your services, it's time to add a service.** I understand you have more seats to fill, but my family of six will likely have a very difficult time finding six seats together. If we don't find them, as guests, we'll assume you don't have space for us.
- **Shift people first before you start adding services.** The shift begins with being more intentional about seating people prior to services with well-trained, friendly greeters and ushers. Then, as one service consistently bumps over 80 percent full, you need to routinely (at least monthly) encourage people to attend the services that have more seats available.
- **Move to multiple services as soon as you have the opportunity.** This move will save you millions of dollars on facility space in the long run. Additionally, you'll create opportunities for people to *attend* a service and *serve* a service. With only one service, it's very challenging to build essential volunteer teams for children's ministry and guest services.

- **Move Sunday school classes so they don't compete with service times.** Don't eliminate Bible studies and Sunday school classes. Just move them to another night. If you don't, there will always be unnecessary competition for space and volunteers. Growing churches maximize the use of their space and volunteers for reaching new people on Sunday morning. After all, that's when new people are most likely to attend a service.

- **Move large student group gatherings to another time during the week.** The objective is to allow students the opportunity to attend a service and serve a service as well. Adding students to your services forces you to program for a younger audience. (As mentioned earlier, that's something most churches need.) It helps you get to critical mass. That adds energy and engagement. Also, getting students to serve is most likely what will keep students engaged in ministry as they transition to adulthood.

- **Avoid starting services before 9:00 A.M. or after 12:00 P.M.** Older people may show up before 9:00 A.M., but you will not reach many young families. If you start services after 12:00 P.M., you'll be competing with many other family and extracurricular activities.

- **Add a third service on Sunday morning before you try another time.** Try 9:00, 10:30, and 11:59 before you add a service on Saturday or Sunday evenings. Yes, you might have to shorten your services to sixty minutes, but that will give you the opportunity to reach more people on Sunday morning. Again, that's when new people are most likely to attend. If you aren't concerned about reaching new people, then don't mess with your service times. Stick with what you're doing.

- **Don't add Saturday or Sunday evening services until you can encourage most staff and volunteers not to come on Sunday morning.** This is particularly a challenge for Saturday evening services. Now that my kids are in school and engaged in activities on Saturdays, I wouldn't work on any church staff or volunteer if you required me to be at services on both Saturday evening and Sunday morning. At least one weekend day needs to be sacred for families.

- **Once you are consistently full on Sunday mornings, you still have options.** Unless you're in a college town, you'll likely get more people to show up on Saturday evening rather than Sunday evening. If you're trying to reach families, know that Sunday evenings will be a challenge. That's when families gear up for the upcoming week. I've seen churches have success with Thursday evening and Monday evening services. You have options, though they aren't ideal.

I've been a part of churches that have sustained five services in one location every weekend for many years. It can be done. Does it take a lot of work? You bet it does. Does it require the staff leaders to build volunteer teams and raise up new leaders so both staff and volunteers don't get burned out? Yep. Does adding new services fuel the momentum and help churches grow? It sure does.

Being proactive about a strategy for growth is the primary reason why every church should be actively planning to add a service, add a campus, or plant a church. Churches in the momentum growth season, however, are not typically mature enough to engage multisite or church planting in a healthy way. Learning how to multiply services, though, is the first step to learning how to multiply locations and new churches.

You Need to Define Your Vision: Create a Picture of the Future That Both Rallies and Repels People

Having a mission statement isn't enough. The mission establishes, in twelve words or less, why you exist. In addition to mission buy-in, though, everyone needs to clearly know *where they are going*. That's the vision.

The vision has to be specific and measurable. It will probably be reflected in several statements that paint a clear picture of where God is taking your church in the future. If you have a solid vision, it will both rally and repel people. You want that, but be wary of three things.

- **Don't confuse your values with your vision.** You can value hospitality, but hospitality isn't a vision for the future.
- **Don't confuse your strategy with your vision.** You can embrace authentic worship as part of your strategy, but authentic worship is not a vision for the future.
- **Don't confuse your doctrine with your vision.** You can believe in biblical authority, but biblical authority is not a vision for the future.

What does this look like? Let me give you some examples.

The Unstuck Group worked with Cross Timbers Community Church in Argyle, Texas. Part of their vision includes this:

We will open eight additional locations in the next ten years throughout the Dallas-Fort Worth region.

That's specific. That's measurable. It's part of the church's overall vision to connect with young families in their community. Now everyone knows part of their vision is to encourage healthy growth by multiplying their footprint throughout their region.

Here's another example. Mount Ararat Baptist Church in Stafford, Virginia, includes this statement in their vision:

We will raise up three hundred new leaders through an intentional leadership development strategy.

There it is for everyone to see. Now the entire church knows they are committed to leadership development. Both staff and volunteer leaders know it's going to require an intentional strategy. And now there's a target so everyone can monitor the progress toward accomplishing that part of their vision.

Parker Hill Church in Scranton, Pennsylvania, also has a big, bold vision. Pastor Mark Stuenzi routinely talks about raising the spiritual temperature in their part of the state. Because "everyone matters" (using their language), they believe God is calling them to reach ten thousand people for Jesus Christ throughout northeastern Pennsylvania.

That's specific. That's measurable. And because they believe God is calling them to reach ten thousand people for Jesus Christ, everything they do today reflects that vision.

To explain this clearly, many churches have a mission statement, core values, and a strategy for discipleship, such as Love God. Grow Christ followers. Serve others.

Very few churches, however, have a clear, bold vision for where they are going in the future. Frankly, I think a key reason leaders don't go there is because clear vision also creates accountability. If there's not a clear goal, then we can continue to do what we've always done and pray and hope for different results. That's the easier and more comfortable path.

A solid vision helps an organization in many ways. If done right, it achieves the following four goals:

- Clarifies the direction of the organization
- Pursues a preferred future
- Inspires people to engage
- Makes it easier to define what the organization *won't* do

For those who believe they have already established a solid vision for the future, let me offer the following test to determine whether or not your organization has clearly defined and communicated its vision. As I've shared previously, these are two surefire ways to know whether or not you've accomplished the goal.

- **A clear vision that is properly communicated will rally people.** People will look at the present situation and agree that there's a better future to be pursued. People will give their time, energy, prayer, financial resources, talents, and gifts to help accomplish that vision. Lots of people will do that. *If people aren't attracted to your church, your vision either isn't strong enough or it hasn't been communicated clearly.*

- **A clear vision that is properly communicated will repel people.** Think of the most successful businesses or churches—Apple, Starbucks, Walmart, Willow Creek, Saddleback, Billy Graham, etc. Each of these businesses or ministries has experienced huge success. If you were to google the names of each of these organizations and the word *haters*, you'll also find there are plenty of people who consider these organizations evil. Clarifying your vision will help some people determine that they don't want to be a part of your cause. (And don't be surprised if some attack.) *Remember, if people aren't leaving your church, your vision either isn't strong enough or it hasn't been communicated clearly.*

I want to challenge you to think about the future vision for your ministry. Does it rally people to your cause? Does it also repel some people? Of course, a healthy vision worth pursuing will attract many more people than it turns away; however, a strong vision will always help some people determine if this church is not for them. You want that.

In other words, if your sense is that you have a vision that makes everyone happy, it's likely you do not have a strong vision.

Skip the Core Values and Develop Team Values: The Culture of Your Church Will Be a Reflection of the Values of Your Team

When I'm working with a church to plan for the future, I facilitate a conversation to develop a clear mission, vision, strategy, and values. These are foundational to developing a focused plan. Let me recap the differences between these foundational statements.

Mission

The mission, which I highlighted in the chapter about the launch season, defines the primary purpose for the church. Typically, in twelve words or less, I help the church develop a mantra that answers the why question. Why do we exist? For The Unstuck Group, as an example, that statement is pretty simple: "We help churches get unstuck." That's why we do what we do.

Vision

The vision, which we just covered, paints a picture of where the church is going in the future. I like to develop that vision for three to five years out. I also like to make the vision specific and measurable. Sometimes it includes actual numerical targets. Other times it names a specific initiative that the church hopes to complete. As long as it's realistically possible with a move of God, bigger vision is always better.

Strategy

The strategy statement clarifies how the mission and vision will be accomplished. The entire chapter on the strategic growth season of the life cycle addresses this topic. Generally, though, I tackle strategy development in two parts. First, I help the church confirm its growth engines. I make sure the church has defined how it will grow by reaching more people and how it will help people grow spiritually. Ideally, the same core strategies will accomplish both the numerical and spiritual growth. Second, I help churches determine what's important *now*. I take the big picture and help them break it into bite-sized chunks to prioritize what needs to happen in the next six to twelve months. I want everyone to understand that this is what I'm supposed to be focused on today.

Values

And that brings me to the values. The values reflect the underlying principles that shape the culture of the church. If developed properly, they should really set the church apart from every other church in the region. They should drive the actions and decisions of every person on the team. I say "should" because churches struggle at times to craft value statements that will really have impact. Instead, they tend to make one of the following mistakes, leading to ineffective results:

1. **They try to name all their values rather than narrowing the list to a set of core values.** More than six or seven core values is too many. Three to five is ideal. When the list is too long, values become watered down. A long list also makes it much harder for everyone to remember and implement the values in every situation.

2. **They copy another church's values.** If I had a nickel for every church that includes one of Willow Creek Community Church's values in their own core values (namely, "We believe excellence honors God and inspires people"), I'd be a very rich church consultant. I love Willow Creek. Bill Hybels has significantly shaped my view of leadership and ministry. But copying Willow Creek's core values won't make your church like Willow Creek.

3. **They don't identify values that are distinctive.** Instead, churches name values that every church embraces. "We believe in the Bible" or "We believe in prayer." Patrick Lencioni, author of *The Advantage*, defines these as permission-to-play values.[1] If you are a church, you *have*

to value the Bible and prayer. These are not options. If it's in your statement of faith, you don't need to restate it in your core values.

4. **They confuse their strategy with their values.** Some churches include things like "worshiping God" or "small groups" as core values. Those aren't values. They are part of a spiritual formation strategy to help people take their next steps toward Christ. Worship and groups are good things, but they aren't compelling core values that shape personality and culture. Again, if it's part of your spiritual growth strategy, you don't need to restate it in your core values.

For that reason, I've shifted from focusing on overall core values to developing internal values that shape the uniqueness of the team itself. In other words, I'd much rather have a set of strong team values that the staff rallies behind than a long list of benign statements that end up buried on a page of the church's website.

Part of this direction comes from my firm belief that strong culture develops from the inside out. The character and personality of the top leaders will ultimately shape the culture.

With that, I steer churches away from developing a broad set of core values for the church and instead toward developing a narrow list of team values. With this approach, churches seem to be more open to identifying what's truly distinctive about their teams.

- What are the key attributes of anyone who would join the team?
- What attitudes invoke the unique personality of the team?

- What are the core behaviors of staff members that drive the culture of the team?

If that list can be identified, then the health of the team (as well as the health of the church) could really be impacted. That list will shape who's on the team. It will help determine who takes on leadership responsibilities. It will help people make better decisions. It will help prioritize what happens first.

If that list can be identified, the team will establish the culture that eventually pervades the entire church. When that happens, a list of benign value statements on the church website becomes superfluous.

If you want to have a stronger, healthier team, begin by being intentional about the values that shape the unique character of who is on the team. That will become the foundation from which the culture develops. And that supports the church's advancement of its mission, vision, and strategy.

Give Leadership Away: If You Have to Call All the Shots, You Are Not a Leader

My very first non-minimum-wage job was back in college. For twelve months I was the "litter czar" of Piqua, Ohio. That wasn't my real title, but that's what my friends called me. I managed a grant for a litter prevention and recycling program for the city. Needless to say, I was in it more for the experience than I was for eliminating the societal evils of littering.

This was my first taste of local government management. Eventually I would finish my business and graduate degrees in public administration and work my way up the career path to become a city manager. But in Piqua, Ohio, I started out as the litter czar.

There are many leadership lessons I could share about that first experience working for the city of Piqua. I could talk about intentionally creating opportunities for young leaders. I could talk about how my first office was in a closet in the back of the building—I had to start from the bottom and work my way up in local government.

Today, though, I want to tell you about my boss, Tom Zechman. He was in charge of the engineering and public works department for the city. He had many responsibilities for managing people and public improvement projects. He was a busy man, but he was never too busy for me.

Tom is a quality leader. He has a sharp mind. He knows how to get things done through his team. The city accomplished a number of significant projects during his tenure.

That said, and I know this to be true, if you were to search the annals of history in the fair city of Piqua, you would find no mention of my twelve-month stint as the litter czar. Yet Tom always had time for me.

I can't recall the specifics of the crisis litter prevention and recycling decisions I had to make in those days, but I do remember that Tom's door was always open. It didn't matter what he was doing, he would stop and give me his full attention. And even though my trashy conundrums were a low priority for him, he would patiently help me figure out my next steps without making the decisions for me.

It was the first example of working for a servant leader I had ever encountered. It was my first experience of being empowered. It was the first opportunity I had to be mentored as a leader.

People ask me how to take steps in their leadership. If you're serious about that, you need to find a Tom Zechman. You need to get a job working for a leader who will model servant leadership. The job isn't what's important. Serving under a servant leader is what's important.

Then, when you probably don't think you're ready to mentor someone else because you're still learning yourself, you have to find a young punk who is just getting started in leadership and life. Set him up in a closet office. Give him grunt work, but also give him your time.

This sounds easy, but it's going to require a significant change in your leadership. You will need to be intentional about giving leadership away. Many pastors of growing churches are unwilling to do this. One of the primary reasons is because there's security in being needed. A good example of this is a leader's addiction to solving problems.

When someone brings a leader a problem, he or she begins to salivate. The leader's mind races through previous experiences to identify instances when this issue was conquered in the past. The leader will identify the solution that worked the last time and relay it to the team. The team appreciates the leader's wisdom and experience. The leader feels valued. Everyone wins.

Then, over time, the number and magnitude of the problems grow. It's exhilarating, because leaders are addicted to solving problems. Eventually, though, the problems become overwhelming. The leader becomes the bottleneck. The growth slows down because the leader can't respond to everything.

Worse yet, the strongest leaders start to leave the team. This addiction to problem solving has elevated the role of manager and pushed the real leaders away. That's what happens when you reward the capacity to identify and deliver problems rather than identify and deliver solutions.

Here's a little trick that will help you to empower others and give leadership away. This is a process to help your team move from a problem-focused team to a solutions-focused team.

1. **Step One: "I bring you the problem."** Your team brings you a problem. Send them away and encourage them to come back with three or four solutions to the problem. When they return with their proposed solutions, encourage them to explain which solution they would choose. Then pick the solution you think is best.

2. **Step Two: "I bring you options for a solution."** Your team learns to bring you solutions rather than problems. Whenever that happens, encourage them again to explain which solution they would choose. When you agree with their solution, have them implement it.

3. **Step Three: "I bring you options and a recommended solution."** Your team learns to bring you solutions and a recommendation for a solution. By now, they've learned how to process decisions within the framework of your mission, values, and strategies. Assuming you agree with their recommendation, encourage them to make it happen.

4. **Step Four: "I process options on my own and implement the best solution."** Your team learns to identify the problem, processes options to solve the problem, and selects the best solution. They communicate to you what happened and how they solved the problem. If it worked, you reinforce that behavior by affirming their

leadership. If it failed, you coach them and encourage them to continue to take those types of risks moving forward.

This is a picture of how we move from managing people to leading people. This is an example of moving from delegating tasks to empowering people to make decisions and implement solutions.

Are you feeling overwhelmed? Are you sensing you have the weight of every decision on your shoulders? Then it's time to start at step one above and begin to raise up and empower other leaders to move your mission forward.

Don't Neglect the Health of Your Soul: God Will Not Bless Your Ministry If You Don't Honor the Sabbath

One of the characteristics of churches in this season of the life cycle is that they experience incredible growth. It's a wonderful challenge, but with that growth, it's not unusual for the pace of ministry to also increase. At first, there will be only occasional times when it's "all hands on deck" and everyone is working hard to meet certain seasonal demands. Then, without any warning signs, those seasons will begin to run into each other. Before you know it, the hurried pace of life without any real downtime becomes the norm.

That's a dangerous moment for any Christ follower, and church leaders are certainly not immune to it. We were designed for renewal. That renewal is needed to maintain a healthy body, mind, and soul. That's why we see God establishing a rhythm from the very beginning of creation that models a time of work followed by a season of rest. We see that again in the Ten Commandments, and again in how Jesus lived out his time on earth. Don't fall for the false sense of security that if you're doing the work of God, you don't have to nurture the health of your soul.

In his book *Soul Keeping: Caring for the Most Important Part of You*, John Ortberg, the senior pastor of Menlo Park Presbyterian Church in Menlo Park, California, shares some advice he received from his mentor, Dallas Willard:

> The main thing you will give your congregation—just like the main thing you will give to God—is the person you become. If your soul is unhealthy, you can't help anybody. You don't send a doctor with pneumonia to care for patients with immune disorders. You, and nobody else, are responsible for the well-being of your own soul.[2]

I've been facilitating leadership coaching networks for many years. These are small gatherings of ten to twelve pastors from all parts of the country. There's typically a mix of lead pastors and other senior leaders from church staff teams. We meet one day a month for six consecutive months.

For the last several years, we've concluded the very first gathering with the same reading assignment. I ask everyone to come back the second month having read *Replenish: Leading from a Healthy Soul*, by Lance Witt. We'll spend all of our other gatherings talking about leadership principles and ministry strategies. There will be lots of conversation about preaching, volunteers, worship, discipleship, biblical stewardship, and much more. I always begin with health of the leader's soul.

I do this because I know myself. I know that my strength and my success as a leader begins with my relationship with Jesus. I also do this because I've lived life long enough to see the consequences of sin. I found out recently that yet another friend had disqualified himself for ministry because of sexual sin. The list of people in my life who have made similar mistakes is now more than twenty church leaders.

All of these stories remind me that I'm one stupid decision from being in the same situation. They remind me that temptations, especially sexual temptations, are something we all face. They remind me that we worship a God who offers second chances. But they also remind me that we need to be taking intentional next steps to protect our marriages, our families, our leadership, our ministries, and most important, the health of our souls.

Lance said it this way: "It's scary to realize that the path to external success and internal emptiness can be the same road."[3]

That's the challenge leaders face in this momentum growth season. The church can very well be experiencing external success, with growth in attendance and people experiencing salvation in Jesus Christ. At the same time, the pace of ministry and life can produce internal emptiness.

As pastors in the church, we have accountability not only for our own health but also for creating an environment conducive to health for our staff and volunteer teams. There needs to be a warning light that goes on when a church is overprogrammed and overscheduled. In other words, you need to have some intentional checkpoints scheduled along the way to monitor the pace and the health of your team.

Ironically, it's typically the smaller churches we serve that struggle most in this area. Particularly when The Unstuck Group is facilitating one of our staffing and structure reviews, one of the areas we assess with the staff team is life balance. There's not a magic formula to assess this, but we do try to discern whether or not their pace of life is healthy.

In those instances when the church needs to establish new disciplines to model health in this area, we recommend the church establish written guidelines for four types of time off:

1. **Day Off Each Week.** Everyone deserves a Sabbath every week. It's a biblical principle. In fact, you may want to consider closing the offices and not allowing *any* ministry events one day each week. That way both the staff and your volunteers get a day off. Chick-fil-A has modeled this for years by being closed on Sundays. Churches are not able to close on Sunday, but is there any reason why we can't choose to close and model the Sabbath on another day of the week?

2. **Vacation Time.** Every staff person should be required to take a minimum of a full week of vacation at least a couple of times during the year. Not only will that offer time for renewal for the staff, but it will require equipping others to carry on ministry when the staff is away. When that happens, you begin to reproduce ministry and leadership in others. That's a good thing. Don't let staff carry vacation forward. Make them use it.

3. **Weekends Off.** In addition to vacation time, during the week, you need to identify how many weekends the staff should take time off. Not all of these weekends should be vacation. Set aside some weekends for the staff to be at the church, but only in observing roles. This fresh perspective will help everyone. Also set aside some weekends for the staff to visit other churches.

This will be a great opportunity to glean new ideas and catch a new vision.

4. **Establish Boundaries for Protecting Evenings.** I recommend you set a maximum number of evenings that staff can be engaged in ministry activities. I prefer two evenings each week, three at the most. And, yes, the staff needs to make sure volunteers hold to these same standards.

Let me state the obvious: some churches will have to assess the number of ministries, programs, and events they're doing in order to implement the healthy boundaries that will protect staff and volunteers. That needs to happen. Your ministry will grow stronger and healthier in the long run if you do that. We'll talk more about that when we begin to address the downslope of the life cycle.

If your team is running at a rapid pace, you need to establish these guidelines in writing. Hold one another accountable. Reward a smart pace of life. This is one of those areas you have to be intentional and proactive about protecting. If you don't address this, you will naturally drift to becoming overworked and overtired, and you'll never get to experience the success and impact of churches that move to a season of sustainable health.

We covered a lot of ground in this chapter on momentum growth. During this season of the life cycle, it's important to prioritize expanding space for growth, clarifying the vision, establishing team values, giving leadership away, and caring for your soul. Just so you know, these momentum growth seasons typically don't last long. It would be unusual to see a church grow by 20 percent, much less double in size, year after year. When it happens, though, it's worth celebrating and giving God praise for building his church. If you handle the mission well during the season of momentum growth, it will prepare you for the strategic growth season that comes next.

CHAPTER 3

STRATEGIC GROWTH
Plan Your Work and Work Your Plan

Many of you just read the subtitle to this chapter and want to stop reading. From your perspective, the subtitle includes a four-letter word. It's the *P* word: *plan*. In your mind, that means slow down and look backward before you can look forward. It means pausing to assess what's working and what needs improvement. It means taking your foot off the pedal for a moment to discern what's next for the church. It means taking a break to make sure we have the right people in the right roles to tackle the right initiatives and get the right results. All of that takes time, and the way you're wired makes slowing down to plan the next steps a huge challenge.

Let's face it. You had a plan before, but it was in your head. You didn't ask for anyone else's input when you developed that plan because you were the only person around at the time. Since then, growth has happened naturally. And that's the problem. Now there are more people. More leaders. More opinions. More ministries. More opportunities. Growth leads to more. And more, if unchecked, leads to complexity and plateau. Don't believe me? Ask the churches on the other side of the life cycle. They're dealing with the consequences of complexity.

Every stage of the life cycle is challenging, but this particular stage is most challenging for entrepreneurs. You are starters. You lead by intuition. If you are a church planter or you've had success transitioning churches in the past, I'm talking to you. In fact, as you read through the two chapters on the launch and momentum growth stages, you were probably salivating and wanting more. It's innate in you to build something new.

Let me warn you, though, because I've seen it happen so many times: some of you won't make it through this stage. You'll either stop growing as a leader and try to take your church back to what it was in the early days or you'll pull the "I'm a church planter" card and go start something new again. You don't have to do that. Your church needs your entrepreneurial bent and will benefit from that in the long run, but your church also needs you to make a leadership shift.

If the first two stages of the life cycle were more intuitive, this next stage is all about being more intentional. In the early days, this isn't necessary because you are in every meeting and every decision of any consequence. As the church grows, however, it becomes impossible for one person to be everywhere and to control everything.

I used that word *control* on purpose. That's the big leadership shift that's required to generate strategic growth. You have to give up control. If you want to continue growing, you have to release ministry, leadership, decision making, and just about everything else to others. A church can't continue to grow on the shoulders of just one person. God didn't design it that way. Instead, he purposely designed us to be a reflection of the entire body of Christ, namely, every person has a gift and a part in the mission of the church. In other words, your gut intuition, which others don't have, must be translated into intentional strategies, systems, and structures to support future health and growth.

That's why Christ Fellowship in West Palm Beach, Florida, determined they couldn't just continue to add ministry programs and events to the calendar. They had to develop an intentional strategy to maintain a focus on essentialism that could be replicated at all their locations.

That's why First Baptist Simpsonville near Greenville, South Carolina, determined people wouldn't connect themselves into small group environments. They had to develop an intentional strategy to encourage biblical community and foster healthy relationships.

That's why Cokesbury United Methodist Church in Knoxville, Tennessee, determined they couldn't continue to take a traditional approach to children's and student ministries. They had to establish an intentional strategy to approach family ministry from birth through graduation by resourcing parents.

That's why Centerpoint Church in Murrieta, California, determined they weren't going to drift toward financial health. They had to develop an intentional strategy to encourage contagious generosity.

That's why Milton Keynes Christian Centre in Milton Keynes, United Kingdom, determined their future growth couldn't be sustained in only one location. They had to develop an intentional strategy to replicate their impact in multiple locations through multisite.

That's why Epikos Church in Milwaukee, Wisconsin, determined they couldn't assume people would naturally sign up to serve. They had to develop an intentional strategy to build high-capacity volunteer teams.

That's why Connexus Church in Barrie, Ontario, determined they couldn't wait for millennial leaders to show up. They had to develop an intentional strategy of both faith and leadership development to equip and empower the next generation of leaders.

That's why Stonecreek Church in Milton, Georgia, determined they couldn't just assume people would engage in evangelism. They had to develop an intentional 365 strategy to help people build relationships, share their faith, and celebrate as more than 365 people accepted Christ in the last year.

All these churches have learned that health and growth are bigger than one person. Instead, they're having the challenging conversations to determine: What's our strategy? What systems are needed to support that strategy? What structure is required to engage more people in this next season of growth?

With that introduction, here are some of the characteristics of churches in the strategic growth season:

1. *They shift from personalities to teams.* The challenge, of course, is to retain all that's good about strong, charismatic leadership while learning to release and empower others. The churches that get this right learn to model team-based leadership at the top of the organization.
2. *Growth pains force leaders to think more strategically.* Without this shift, complexity will continue to grow and ministry silos will begin to develop. Focused strategies also help shift from personalities to teams.
3. *They confirm their discipleship path.* This is one of the key strategies that any church needs to define. In small churches, next steps are driven relationally, that is, people develop a relationship that leads to a next step.

As churches grow, people will need to take a step before those relationships develop.

4. *Systems are established to reinforce healthy behaviors.* Rather than rely only on chance, values will inform right decisions every time. Boundaries are established and steps are defined so that decision making can be released to more people.

5. *Structure forms to support future growth.* By structure I mean a combination of lay leadership, church governance, staff leadership, and volunteer ministry teams. In the past, it was "all hands on deck." Everyone did everything. As the church grows, that creates confusion and chaos. It's time to redefine roles and responsibilities.

6. *They begin to flex their healthy change muscles.* While it's still growing, the church needs to learn how to let go of the past and embrace the future. Now is the time to begin establishing this in the culture: change is expected and is a sign of health.

As hard as it may be to grasp, what your church experienced in the previous two stages of the life cycle was relatively easy growth. But this season of the church is going to take work. You can't assume that because it worked in the past, it's going to work now and in the future. Having more people leads to more challenges. That's going to require some changes.

If we are faithful in the little things, though, and God continues to build his church, we may experience a movement that has profound kingdom impact. Let's look at the key changes that will be required to develop strategic growth and will prepare your church for sustained health.

Build a Strategy to Accomplish Your Vision: Good Stewardship Demands a Good Plan of Attack

In my book *Stuck in a Funk?*,[1] I introduced the concept of churches needing to "mind the gap." This concept was birthed out of several visits to London. If you've been there, you're likely familiar with the Tube, the city's subway system. Wherever you travel using the subway in London, you're always told to mind the gap. You hear that phrase on the loudspeakers. You see that phrase plastered throughout the subways. That warning to mind the gap is everywhere. The gap refers to the space between the subway platform and the train. It would be a bad day if you fell in *that* gap.

I think a gap exists in churches as well. For years I've warned church leaders to mind the gap. For churches, the gap is the void between the vision and the people who are waiting to do ministry in order to accomplish the vision. These churches, particularly growing churches, have already clarified their vision. Because of that, no one questions *where* the leadership is hoping to take the church in the future. The gap exists around *how* the church is going to get there. That *how* void is filled by strategy.

I think of strategy as the plan of attack. It's the combination of initiatives and tactics that the team will run to achieve the win.

Without defining a strategy to accomplish vision, churches typically drift back to doing what they've always done. Because Sunday is always coming, that tends to get the most focus. The urgency of today will always be louder than the desired destination for the future.

In his book *The E-Myth Revisited*, Michael Gerber wrote, "What makes people work is an idea worth working for, along with a clear understanding of what needs to be done."[2] The ideas worth working for are your mission and vision. The mission answers the question of why you exist; the vision addresses where you are headed. The "clear understanding of what needs to be done" is addressed by your strategy, which puts legs to the vision.

Here's what strategic planning means to me:

- You set aside time to get perspective.
- You honestly answer the question of where you are now by looking at external and internal patterns and trends.
- You plan for the future. You answer the question of where you're headed. You establish or confirm mission, vision, and team values.
- You define or redefine your core strategies. You get your whole team on the same page as to how you are planning to align your time, energy, and resources to the vision.
- You map out how you will put your plans into action by asking what's important now. You empower your current team and identify gaps that need to be filled by volunteers or near-term hires.
- You build accountability with action plan leaders, dates, and deadlines.

If your eyes are beginning to glaze over, I get it. This conversation is particularly challenging for entrepreneurs and visionaries. The reality is that you may not be wired to deliver this. This requires unique gifting and a lot of focus and hard work.

Let me explain it this way. I believe there are three types of leaders. Some leaders have an ability to clarify and cast a vision for the future. Other leaders can execute; they can build a team of people to get things done. Still other leaders, those who are strategically wired, are able to connect the dots between the two. They are uniquely gifted to map out the plans to help an organization get from here to there. It's very uncommon for one leader to be wired to lead at all three levels. You may need to find someone else to take the lead when it comes to developing strategy.

This, though, is the key to moving forward when momentum growth begins to slow or plateau. Strategy provides the intentionality that allows a church to ultimately experience sustained health. And I think this is a stewardship responsibility of every church leader.

Remember Luke 14:28–30:

> But don't begin until you count the cost. For who would begin construction of a building without first calculating the cost to see if there is enough money to finish it? Otherwise, you might complete only the foundation before running out of money, and then everyone would laugh at you. They would say, "There's the person who started that building and couldn't afford to finish it!"

It's not enough to determine we're eventually going to construct a building. (That's the vision.) We have to develop plans for that building. We have to make sure we have the money to build it. We have to hire contractors. We have to manage the project to make sure it gets completed on time and under budget. (That's the strategy.) Without strategy, we invite people to laugh at us and mock us because we're being poor stewards of God's resources.

For a church to find health and continue to grow in this season of the life cycle, the strategy gap needs to be addressed. That likely includes making sure that strategically minded leaders are on the team, engaging the discipline of routinely pulling away to confirm and focus the strategy, and building accountability to manage and monitor the strategy to make sure it's delivering the expected results.

Implement Systems Around Common Touch Points: Don't Let One Person Become a Bottleneck to Helping More People

If strategies are the long-term view of how the vision gets accomplished, then systems are the day-to-day methods for executing the ministry strategy. In fact, for churches, I describe a healthy system as a simple, replicable process to help people move from where they are to where God wants them to be. During the momentum growth phase, these systems start to form, but they're typically handled by one person. Instead of documenting that process in writing and equipping others to share the responsibility, one person becomes the system.

For example, let's consider helping people connect on a serving team. In smaller churches, the system for helping someone volunteer is typically, "Go see Sue." Sue is the volunteer coordinator. The system is in her brain. When someone wants to serve, she does the same thing every time. But she has never put her system down on paper or built a team of people to handle that process so it could increase in scale as the church grows.

During momentum growth, there's no need to create those systems, because the growth and the connections happen naturally. As churches shift into the strategic growth season, though, the number of people increases and so does the number of volunteer connection opportunities. Sue gets overwhelmed. Additionally, new people don't know Sue, so it creates a challenge to help them get connected. This is not a Sue problem; it's a systems problem. The process needs to be documented. A team needs to be built. That team needs to be trained on the system. Then the team needs to be empowered to work the system in Sue's place.

Every church is unique, so it would be impossible for me to list every system every church needs. But let me give you some common examples of systems you will likely need to develop:

- Registering new children and following up with their parents
- Helping guests connect to the church
- Participating in a home group
- Volunteering to serve
- Processing financial gifts and communicating with contributors
- Registering for an event
- Developing new leaders
- Getting something promoted
- Scheduling facility space
- Hiring a new staff person

To build your list of necessary systems, think about the key touch points where you interact with people. These are the instances when someone wants to take a next step. Prioritize the touch points that experience the most interactions and begin there. Those are the places where you need strong systems. If a process happens over and over again, get the process out of one person's brain and onto paper so it can be executed by teams of people now and in the future.

Here are some common characteristics of healthy systems that may help you determine where to start and whether or not you're moving in the right direction:

- **Healthy systems empower leaders to accomplish ministry without always having to get permission.** Without systems, every decision rises to the top of the organization. In your case that may be the senior pastor, the senior leadership team, the church board, or a committee. A good system addresses permissions one time and frees many people to make decisions on their own.
- **Healthy systems are embraced and championed by the top leadership.** This protects the leaders lower in the organization who are implementing the systems. There needs to be buy-in from the top. If there's any hint of some people excluding themselves from following the process, you should stop using it now. But leaders also need to be aware that avoiding systems will eventually cause your church's impact to plateau. You need systems to sustain growth.
- **Healthy systems mobilize more people rather than lean on a handful of talented individuals.** If your system is to contact Mary for more information, you don't have a system; you have a talented Mary. If your system is to go hear Joe teach on the topic, you don't have a system; you have a gifted Joe. Good systems point people to next steps (processes, tools, resources, etc.) rather than specific people.
- **Healthy systems simplify the path.** The objective is to create enough of a framework to streamline the next

steps and make life easier for people. Good systems are intuitive. Typically, the fewer moving parts, the better the system. If you want to improve a system, challenge your team to figure out how to reduce the steps required. And whatever you do, make sure your customer doesn't have to guess where to go next.

- **Healthy systems improve over time.** If you feel like you have to wait until the system is perfect, you will stay stuck. Roll out the system. Test-drive it. See what works and tweak the rest based on the feedback you receive.
- **Healthy systems need to change over time.** This is the challenge many churches on the other side of the life cycle are facing. They're still trying to use systems that worked years ago but are no longer effective today. If you're not careful, the systems (following the rules) can become the focus over accomplishing the mission and vision of the church.

Here's the opportunity that exists if you get the right systems in place: One talented person without a replicable system can help one person at a time. Many people using healthy systems, however, can help many people at one time. If you want to multiply your impact, you have to embrace healthy systems.

Adjust Your Structure to Reflect Your Strategy: Start by Making Sure the Senior Pastor Has a Healthy Span of Care

Through the launch and momentum growth seasons of a church, it's not unusual for everyone on the staff ministry team to be directly connected to the senior pastor. The organization stays very flat. As the team grows, however, the senior pastor has to supervise and lead more and more people. Over time, it becomes a span of care challenge.

In business, this concept is called a span of control. It's a way of identifying how many people one person directly supervises. In ministry, I prefer describing this as the span of care. Care reflects both the leadership needed to help people fulfill their jobs and the mentoring and discipleship needed to encourage them in their spiritual development.

In my experience, a leader's span of care capacity varies. Some people have the capacity to lead two or three others. Some people can lead up to seven or eight. I highly recommend monitoring the overall span of care in your ministry. You can do that by adding the number of volunteers and staff on your team and then dividing by the number of staff and volunteer leaders. If the result is higher than five, you likely have a span of care issue and you need more leaders.

Let's get back to the senior pastor. As the church grows, more staff are hired. I've been to some churches trying to transition from momentum growth to strategic growth, and the senior pastor is trying to lead twelve or more people. This is particularly challenging for a senior pastor because at this point in the life cycle of the church, the senior pastor really has three key roles:

1. Being the primary teacher and communicator
2. Leading the senior staff team
3. Casting the vision for where the church is going next

These are three responsibilities the senior pastor can't delegate to anyone else. With the teaching responsibility requiring ten to twenty hours each week in preparation and delivery, this also constrains the ability to effectively lead too many people.

I've learned that my span of care, for example, is probably no more than five or six. Any more than that, and I may be able to stay on top of their tasks and responsibilities, but I don't know anything else about what's happening in their lives. I don't know what they're celebrating. I don't know their personal challenges. I don't know their desires for the future and how to help them develop as leaders. I don't know how to pray for them. Because of all these factors, having a span of care that's too big not only impacts the leader, it also impacts the people you are trying to lead.

The only way to appropriately address this challenge is to begin to develop additional layers of leadership, beginning with establishing a senior leadership team. Churches hit this transition point at different sizes, but I've found that you feel the need for it when there are more than eight people in a room trying to make a decision.

I refer to this dynamic as the rule of eight. Here's how it works: if a decision is required, the team meeting should be limited to no more than eight people. When there are more than eight people:

- It becomes difficult for everyone to share their ideas.
- People don't ask the questions that need to be asked.
- Decision making slows down.
- It becomes hard to assign ownership to action items.
- People are less likely to fully embrace decisions because they haven't had a chance to provide input.

You can still assemble more than eight people, including pulling the entire team together for all-staff gatherings. Just make sure these aren't decision-making meetings. Use these larger gatherings to share stories, train, cast vision, share key information, and so on. If someone tries to shift the meeting into decision mode, though, call a time-out and take that conversation offline with just the people who need to be involved in the decision.

Count the people in your regular ministry staff meetings. That includes all the pastors and all the ministry directors. As the church grows, this group will eventually exceed eight people. When that happens, the focus naturally shifts to ministry-specific conversations (youth, kids, women's groups, events, etc.). It becomes a kind of representative form of government, where each leader comes to represent their specific ministry area. The conversations about overall church health and spiritual growth get squeezed out. Everyone begins to protect their turf. The meetings are more about execution than they are about vision and strategy.

If you want to continue through the strategic growth phase to sustained health, you must make a key structural transition: you have to begin by inviting only leaders of leaders to this regular team meeting. In other words, you have to reduce the number of people involved in every ministry decision, and you have to develop a senior leadership team.

I'll talk more about who should be on the senior leadership team and the key roles they perform in the chapter on sustained health, but without a doubt, a healthy structure begins with a healthy senior leadership team. Here, let me just state the obvious: this shift moves the leadership off of one person's shoulders so that it is shared by a team.

As you begin to reshape your leadership team, consider the following guidelines to help you develop a healthy structure:

- **Your structure should reflect your strategy to accomplish your vision.** Form follows function. If a strategy is core to reaching more people and helping them take their next step toward Christ, then your structure needs to support it. If you want everyone to be in a group, who will champion that step? If you want everyone to serve, who will champion that step?
- **Your structure should play to the strengths of the people on your team.** Assess the roles that need to be filled along with the way each person is wired. What are the person's gifts and skills? What are their experiences? How does their personality impact their contribution? What are they most passionate about? Finding a good fit makes the team healthier, and each person will be more fulfilled.
- **Your structure should be built around the capacity of the leaders.** I'll share more about this in a moment, but not all leaders are created equal. Some have more capacity than others. I've not found an assessment to determine leadership capacity. It's all based on looking at how a leader has demonstrated leadership capacity in the past. That's the best predictor of how they'll live out their leadership role in the future.
- **Your structure should connect every ministry program to the senior leadership team.** In other words, nothing stands on its own. Particularly in churches, it's not uncommon for ministries or programs to be independent and unconnected to the leadership team. Again, this is why we focus on making sure the structure supports the strategy.

- **Your structure should support future growth.** I like to develop structures that could support the organization if it were twice its current size. This helps to identify future leadership gaps and begins to help the organization prioritize leadership roles as financial resources become available. Doing this helps the church begin to make decisions today that will influence its growth tomorrow.

Let me suggest as well that if you are in a high-growth situation, you may need to review and adjust your structure every one to two years. The key, though, is to make sure you have a process in place to confirm and renew your strategy before you make any adjustments to your structure.

Clarify the Discipleship Path: Keeping People Busy in Ministry Activities Doesn't Produce Spiritual Growth

Over the last several years, Willow Creek Community Church in South Barrington, Illinois, has facilitated an amazing effort to survey more than fifteen hundred churches, including more than half a million churchgoers, about their spiritual growth. The results have been summarized in a number of resources. Of particular interest to me is the book *Move: What 1,000 Churches Reveal About Spiritual Growth* by Greg Hawkins and Cally Parkinson,[3] which highlights the best practices of churches when it comes to spiritual formation.

There are a lot of great learnings for churches in all stages of the life cycle, but this book may be of most interest to our strategic growth season. These churches are facing a unique challenge, namely, what do we do with all the brand-new Christians? Wouldn't every church leader trade their problems for that one? It's a great problem to have.

With that challenge also comes a huge responsibility. The pastors I encounter in these growing churches sense that weight. As Christ followers, Scripture challenges us to obey our pastors and church leaders, but these same people are accountable to a higher leader as well. "Obey your spiritual leaders, and do what they say. Their work is to watch over your souls, and they are accountable to God" (Heb. 13:17).

Because of this responsibility, pastors and church leaders are constantly wrestling with the task of encouraging believers to take their next steps toward Christ. Most pastors will agree that churches have to offer more than just a worship service on Sunday morning to encourage spiritual formation. But how much more?

In this season of strategic growth, the church will begin to add ministry programming to foster these next steps. That may include Bible studies, spiritual growth classes, home groups, serving opportunities, community outreach projects, mission trips, women's and men's ministries, and so on. The hope, of course, is that adding more ministry programming will offer more opportunities for people to take their next steps. And that will produce more spiritual growth.

So back to the book *Move*. Among the many key insights that Hawkins and Parkinson share is this nugget that is so critical for momentum growth churches:

> Based on findings from the most effective churches, however, this "more is better" way of thinking is not the best route for

people who are new to a church, and it is particularly unsuitable for people who are taking their first steps to explore the Christian faith. . . . Instead of offering a ministry buffet with multiple tempting choices of activities and studies, these churches make one singular pathway a virtual prerequisite for membership and full engagement with the church.[4]

In other words, you will need to add ministry programming to help people take their next steps. But those programs need to be focused. The path needs to be clear.

It's in the strategic growth season that churches are best positioned to make this decision and stick to it. If you do, you will avoid the biggest challenge that declining churches face on the opposite slope of the life cycle, namely, complexity. In these churches, multiple ministries compete for people's time and attention. Churches become bloated over time as new ministry programs are added but nothing is ever taken away. We'll deal with that challenge later on, but the best way to beat ministry bloat is to never allow that complexity to take hold.

Let me push a little harder. When Jesus called the first disciples into ministry, he said, "Come, follow me, and I will show you how to fish for people!" (Matt. 4:19). Let's consider what Jesus *didn't* say when he summoned those first disciples into ministry.

He didn't say, "Come, follow me, and I will teach you spiritual insights!"

He didn't say, "Come, follow me, and I will show you how to sing worship songs together!"

He didn't say, "Come, follow me, and I will gather you together in a home group!"

He didn't say, "Come, follow me, and I will show you how to pray!"

He didn't say, "Come, follow me, and I will make you members of the church!"

I think we can all agree that Jesus was fairly insightful, so I think it's interesting that of all the things he could have said, he chose to put the focus of ministry on reaching other people. It's not that any of the other alternatives is wrong. In fact, we can find plenty of examples in the Gospels where Jesus intentionally taught, prayed, and shared fellowship in small groups with his disciples. But I believe it's important to acknowledge that Jesus did all of that for the purpose of getting these disciples on mission.

Generally, that's not how we disciple people in the church today. Rather than putting the focus of ministry on reaching people, we prioritize different activities. Doesn't it make you wonder if there's something significant about the initial vision that Jesus shared with these first disciples?

Maybe discipleship is really more about helping people serve God by serving others. Maybe it's more about disciples making disciples. Maybe we need to unlearn how we do discipleship in the church.

How would the church look different if we approached the discipleship process as fishing for people? How would it look if, instead of offering a plethora of options to engage, we gave people at various stages of their spiritual journey—from new believer to mature in the faith—a clear next step to take? What if we offered a simple path because we know that spiritual growth steps necessarily require sacrifice and stretching of our faith? That's the opportunity that momentum growth churches have to help shape the spiritual formation of all these new believers.

Increase the Leadership Capacity of Your Team: Leadership Isn't Leadership If It Isn't Released to Others

As I shared earlier, this strategic growth season requires a shift from one leader's gut intuition into intentional strategies, systems, and structures to support future health and growth. In churches there are two facets of strategic growth that are foundational. The first area we've already covered is the discipleship path. That's the strategy to help people take their next spiritual steps. To get to the next phase of the life cycle, though, that's not enough. Sustained health will also require a growing number of leaders. You have to develop a strategy to help people take their next leadership steps as well.

In the Old Testament, we see the foundations of this playing out when Jethro tells Moses to "select from all the people some capable, honest men who fear God and hate bribes. Appoint them as leaders over groups of one thousand, one hundred, fifty, and ten" (Ex. 18:21). In the New Testament, we see this demonstrated when Paul instructed Timothy: "You have heard me teach things that have been confirmed by many reliable witnesses. Now teach these truths to other trustworthy people who will be able to pass them on to others" (2 Tim. 2:2).

We see this model of leadership throughout the Bible where people are entrusting responsibilities with other people to carry on the ministry. Leadership isn't leadership if it isn't released to others. Because of that, it's important to ask: Is my leadership more about getting people to do what I want them to do or helping people be who God designed them to be? Am I entrusting leadership to other capable people or am I just delegating tasks? If I wasn't here, would the ministry continue to grow without me?

It's so contradictory, isn't it? We've been so conditioned to equate leadership with a person. Yet that's not how God created it. In God's design, the sum is greater than the parts. Leadership doesn't rest with one individual; it's entrusted to capable men and women.

Based on what I see in Scripture, I think we can agree that leadership is one of many spiritual gifts. Some have it and some do not. We also know, mostly from the passage in Exodus 18, that there are different levels of leadership capacity. I've created this picture of the leadership pathway to help us identify different leadership capacities:

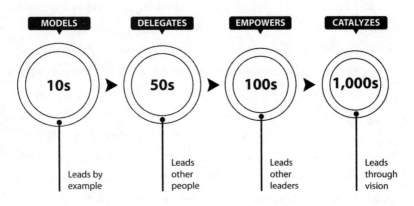

One key distinctive of churches in the strategic growth phase of the life cycle is that they've developed an intentional strategy to identify, develop, and grow the number of leaders at every level. As we invest in these leaders, we're helping them to develop spiritually. We're helping them to grasp the unique vision, strategy, and values that shape the church. We're also helping them to learn the new leadership competencies that are required to lead at each of these levels. Here are some examples of the competencies required at each level of leadership.

- **Leaders of tens lead by example.** They model for others the way things should be done. This is an important approach to leadership when a new ministry launches. During this season, leaders have to do most of the work themselves. This helps to establish a foundation for the future. "Leading by doing" gives leaders the opportunity to shape the team values and strategy of the church. Key competencies include:
  1. Developing your personal mission and goals
  2. Leading from your strengths
  3. Practicing personal disciplines
  4. Modeling a bias for action
  5. Managing your time, including work-life balance
- **Leaders of fifties lead other people.** They delegate tasks effectively to share the workload. The leader learns to recruit other people to join the ministry team. Rather than doing all the work on their own, they begin to delegate tasks and responsibilities to other people. The leader still owns the responsibility for making things happen, but they're including other people in the effort. Key competencies include:
  1. Setting clear expectations
  2. Managing conflict
  3. Communicating effectively with the team
  4. Building teams of volunteers
  5. Discipling other people
- **Leaders of hundreds lead other leaders.** They empower others to make decisions and take responsibility for accomplishing the mission and vision. Instead of a hands-on role, where they're on top of all the tasks, they

shift to a role where they're really concerned about leading, caring for, and raising up other leaders. They don't give up their responsibility for the outcome, but they begin to release team building and decisions of execution to other people. Key competencies include:

1. Measuring and evaluating for results
2. Developing and mentoring leaders
3. Dealing with underperformers and dysfunction
4. Stewarding people, time, and money
5. Planning for the future

- **Leaders of thousands lead through the vision.** They catalyze a movement around a single focused purpose and strategy. They consistently prioritize the overall health of the church. Rather than a ministry-specific focus, they have a global perspective that encompasses every aspect of the organization. These folks are leading other leaders, but they also have influence that reaches beyond their direct reports. They are coming alongside the senior leader to champion the vision that God has given the church. Key competencies include:

1. Casting vision
2. Developing a senior leadership team
3. Renewing vision and strategy
4. Leading change
5. Shaping culture

Let me state the obvious: you will need far more leaders of tens than you will need leaders of thousands. But you will need every capacity of leadership to sustain health in the long run. With that, I challenge you to put together a strategy to help leaders grow.

Don't just tack on a leadership development program. Your church doesn't need another program. Instead, identify a development strategy that can be embedded into your existing ministries. That may mean, for example, that small group and ministry team leaders are plugged into coaching relationships that help them not only engage in ministry but also grow in their leadership.

This chapter has been all about planning before you build. In it, I challenged you to think about developing a strategy, implementing systems, confirming your structure, clarifying your discipleship path, and establishing a process for developing leaders. Growth in this season demands stewardship. In other words, you have to be intentional about developing a strategy and putting that plan into action. If you steward this well, my prayer is that you will experience the sustained health that follows.

CHAPTER 4

SUSTAINED HEALTH

Becoming the Church God Designed It to Be

We're finally at the pinnacle of the life cycle. In this stage, I want to talk about sustained health; however, I'm going to approach this chapter a little differently than the others. In the previous chapters and the ones that follow, the focus is on what churches should be *doing* to become healthy. I don't want to do that here. Instead, I want to offer a picture of sustained health. Why? If I just stop at what healthy churches are doing, you might start checking boxes and determine you've done it all, so you must be leading a healthy church. That may or may not be the case.

Some of you might take issue with some of the tactics. You might disagree and argue that churches can be healthy without engaging the strategies I've highlighted. You have your own perspective of what healthy churches should be doing. You might be right, and I very well could be wrong. But at the end of the day, I don't care who is right or wrong, because the ministry tactics aren't the win. I'm much more concerned about outcomes. I'm more interested in results. I want more churches to be healthy, and I want the church to become everything God designed it to be.

Very little is written about the outcomes of healthy churches.

Instead, you'll find many articles and books on inputs, namely, what healthy churches should be doing. I realize I certainly deserve part of the blame for this. That's been the focus of much of my writing as well. I have a picture in my mind of what a healthy church should look like, but I can't presume others have that same picture.

For example, I completed an online search on the "characteristics of healthy churches." Much of the writing I found focused on tactics rather than outcomes. The articles suggested churches should be *doing* things like:

- Worshiping with a God-exalting style
- Preaching gospel-centered messages
- Implementing small-groups ministry
- Praying corporately
- Engaging an evangelism strategy
- Structuring around biblical eldership
- Developing servant leaders
- Practicing the sacraments
- Loving one another through Christian fellowship
- Clarifying the vision
- Mobilizing volunteers based on their gifts
- Encouraging a missional mind-set

There are some very good practices in that list. I'm confident that some would approach these practices differently than I. Some would argue the list isn't prioritized the right way. Some would make the case that other key practices are missing. The point is, it's a list of tactics, not necessarily the characteristics of a healthy church.

As I said, I can't presume others have the same picture of a healthy church as I, and you shouldn't either. In fact, there's a good chance that others in your church and on your ministry team have different perspectives than you. This is one area where there should be both clarity and unity. Everyone should know what the win looks like, and everyone should be pulling in the same direction.

When I'm working with a church to focus their vision and strategy for the future, this is one of the exercises we go through as a team. I try to help teams come to an agreement on the outcomes required to monitor whether or not the church is experiencing health. My hope is that this process will generate a new focus on praying for and pursuing health rather than just "doing church."

With that, let me offer these characteristics of what I'm hoping churches will experience in this stage of sustained health:

1. *They are growing over time.* By no means does this mean the size of the church is a reflection of health. This is just an acknowledgment that when the church is healthy, it grows. We see this in the descriptions of the earliest days of the New Testament church. My hope is that your church, with the encouragement of the Holy Spirit, will also grow in numbers.

2. *They are unified.* There's a unity of purpose. There's a unity of direction. In fact, there's so much alignment and focus that it's acknowledged not only within the leadership and congregation but also by those from the outside looking in. It's impossible to experience sustained health if there's division within the church.

3. *They are bearing good fruit.* We are reminded in Scripture that healthy trees produce good fruit. Because of that,

the first thing I look for when assessing the health of a church is whether or not it's producing fruit. Primarily, I'm hoping to see new disciples of Jesus. Churches that are experiencing sustained health are consistently baptizing and teaching new disciples.

4. *The ministry is multiplying.* That will look different in different churches, but multiplication will happen. New ministry leaders will be developed. New home groups will launch. New campuses will open. New churches will be planted. The iterations of this multiplication will certainly be unique, depending on the size and location of the church, but God designed the church to multiply everywhere: in Jerusalem, throughout Judea, in Samaria, and to the ends of the earth.

5. *They embrace new.* They expect change. Churches experiencing sustained health know that God is renewing every Christ follower, and thus, his church must constantly be renewing as well. As hard as some churches try, it's impossible to put new wine in old wineskins.

6. *They are generous.* The people of the church are generous, and the church itself is generous. Churches experiencing sustained health learn to be wise stewards of all their resources in order to be prepared for whatever God may have next. There's an abundance mind-set, because churches that practice generosity learn that God always provides.

Is a church that has God-exalting worship, gospel-centered messages, and corporate prayer healthy? Maybe. Maybe not. Those strategies certainly help produce health, but they're not necessarily guarantees of good health.

Is a church that is experiencing one of the six characteristics I've outlined above healthy? Maybe. Maybe not. Any one of those characteristics on its own may not be a reflection of total health. If we find a church with all those characteristics, though, it's very likely the church is positioned for sustained health.

Confirm the Ministry Is Bearing Good Fruit: Your Ministry Strategy Should Produce New Disciples of Jesus

I'm fortunate to have the opportunity to serve churches with a variety of ministry approaches and philosophies. Because I facilitate next steps rather than prescribing a specific ministry approach, I get to help many different types of churches. Based on that experience, I can confirm that many different strategies work. In fact, if someone claims to have the one way to grow a healthy church, you should probably turn and run in the other direction.

I've also been engaged in different roles in church ministry for more than two decades. During that time I've seen different iterations of ministry strategies from the seeker model to purpose-driven to cell-based to emergent to missional and more. In my opinion, some of those strategies work better than others, but I've also seen healthy, growing churches that embrace versions of all those strategies. By the same token, just because you use a seeker, attractional model doesn't mean you have a healthy church. And just because your church leans missional doesn't mean it's necessarily healthy either.

Regardless of the strategy you use, one sign of health is the fruit the ministry produces. Jesus reminded us: "A good tree produces good fruit, and a bad tree produces bad fruit. A good tree can't produce bad fruit, and a bad tree can't produce good fruit" (Matt. 7:17–18).

So, what is the fruit we should be watching for to confirm if our tree is healthy? It would be good for you and your team to come to agreement on that question, but I'm assuming one type of good fruit would be new disciples of Jesus. After all, Jesus's final challenge to his followers was to "Go and make disciples of all the nations, baptizing them in the name of the Father and the Son and the Holy Spirit. Teach these new disciples to obey all the commands I have given you. And be sure of this: I am with you always, even to the end of the age" (Matt. 28:19–20).

Let me state the obvious here. We're supposed to make *new* disciples. We're supposed to baptize and teach *new* disciples. That, at the very least, is part of the good fruit. What that suggests is that if a group of thousands of people gathers for worship and teaching on Sunday, but the church is not producing new disciples, that church is not healthy. If a church is effectively connecting almost everyone who attends worship into home groups or Sunday school classes or Bible studies, but it's not producing new disciples, that church is not healthy. If people gather for worship and then scatter missionally into the community to share the gospel, but the ministry isn't producing new disciples, that church is not healthy.

Again, the win isn't the strategy the church uses, though I hope I effectively persuaded you in the last chapter on strategic growth that you need a strategy. My challenge here is that you don't celebrate the strategy. I want you to celebrate the good fruit.

Stonecreek Church in Milton, Georgia, took this challenge seriously. They launched a 365 Campaign based on the picture of the early church in Acts. During the campaign, they were praying specifically that 365 people would be saved. The number was based on one person representing one day of the total year. This was a big prayer for a church of just over 1,200 people.

Every time someone accepted Christ, they lit a lightbulb on a giant 365 sign in the lobby. That visual was powerful for the church, and it kept the priority in front of them for the entire twelve months.

Pastor Steven Gibbs described the initiative this way: "We want to be a daily type of church—a church that moves church beyond Sunday and into the everyday lives of people. We want to mobilize people to create lasting change in the world daily."

With that in mind, the leadership team prayed about the campaign and solicited every Stonecreek volunteer to pray with them as well. The whole staff team met twice a week to pray. They also communicated regularly with the church throughout the campaign, including sharing stories of people turning on lightbulbs to acknowledge their new faith in Jesus.

You can celebrate along with Stonecreek, because last Easter they reached their goal of seeing 365 people accept Christ. I love that intentionality and focus around fulfilling God's vision of people being saved daily. You might argue with their strategy, but it produced fruit—good fruit.

This good-fruit philosophy can be applied to help you and your team make all kinds of decisions for the future. Is someone ready to step into a leadership role? Is his or her life producing good fruit? Do we launch a new ministry program? Do we know what type of good fruit we expect? If so, will the new ministry produce it? Should we continue offering an all-church event that we've done for the past several years? Is the event still producing good fruit? If you ever run into a situation where something's not producing good fruit, it's time to prune that branch so the tree can regain health.

Pursue Health and Growth Over Time: If the Church Is Healthy, It Will Continue to Grow

If a church is producing fruit, then I'm confident there will also be growth over time. Rick Warren, pastor of Saddleback Church in Lake Forest, California, said, "All living things grow if they're healthy. You don't have to make them grow—it's just natural for living organisms."[1] I agree. Healthy things grow. And so should healthy churches.

That's exactly what we see in the description of the early church in the book of Acts. In chapter 2 we get a picture of all the things the church was doing. That included teaching and fellowship. They prayed together. They were generous with one another. They worshiped together. They celebrated the Lord's Supper together. That's a picture of their discipleship strategy. Because of that, the church was healthy. What was the result? "Each day the Lord added to their fellowship those who were being saved" (Acts 2:47). People were added to the fellowship, and the church grew.

It didn't stop there. The ministry continued to expand throughout the region. The church "became stronger as the believers lived in the fear of the Lord. And with the encouragement of the Holy Spirit, it also grew in numbers" (Acts 9:31). Once again, the church continued to grow. I'm glad it did; otherwise, I wouldn't be a Christ follower today.

That's the kind of story that motivates me to do what I do. I want churches to develop vision and strategy for experiencing health. Then I want those healthy churches to grow. I pray for churches to grow. I pray for churches to have a bigger impact in the communities they serve. I pray for more people to experience the forgiveness, hope, and purpose only available through a relationship with Jesus. In this case, *more* is definitely better.

Now, let me be clear again. I'm not suggesting that big churches are always healthy churches. I'm also not trying to make the case that small churches are necessarily always unhealthy. I *am* making the case, though, that healthy churches should grow.

But I can still hear the naysayers begging to differ. One might argue, "The church won't grow because it's in a rural location." Another might push back, "The church won't grow because it's in a small community." Still another might say, "The church won't grow because there are too many other churches for people to attend." Or it's in the Northeast. Or it's in the Northwest. Or a megachurch built a huge campus just down the road.

I may have been persuaded by arguments like that in the past, but then I visited Paradise. I'm talking about Paradise, Texas. This city, and I use that term loosely, has a population of only 468 people.[2] Paradise, if you haven't been there, wasn't exactly paradise for me. After the hour-long drive from Dallas, I felt as if I were in the middle of nowhere. There's a school, a post office, one intersection with a traffic light, and a large church.

Grace Fellowship Church is pastored by BJ Rutledge. The church in Paradise started in 2003 with only ten families and their friends. Now they have more than thirteen hundred people gathering for worship every weekend. That's nearly three times the size of the community where they're situated. BJ and the leadership team have never let their rural, small-town community be a barrier to reaching more people for Jesus. In fact, they have a vision to expand the church's impact in other small, rural communities.

I'm glad they have that vision, because there's a lot of opportunity in Wise County, Texas, where Paradise is situated. Though there are more than one hundred churches in Wise County, as of 2010 almost 60 percent of the county is unchurched.[3] Unfortunately, the churches are losing ground here just as they are in many other locations across the country. In 1990, less than half the county was unchurched.[4] In other words, as more people moved into the county, fewer people connected with a church.

Paradise is unique for many reasons, but there is one way it's like every community I visit to help churches get unstuck. The community may be rural, urban, or suburban. The community could be a village, town, city, or metropolis. It doesn't matter where I go. I'm going to find people outside the faith and outside the church.

For example, I live smack-dab in the middle of the Bible Belt near Atlanta, Georgia. If any community is overchurched, it's where I live. It feels like there's a church on every corner. Yet, according to the Association of Religion Data Archives, only one out of every four of my neighbors is connected to a church.[5] The need for healthy, growing churches is everywhere.

There's no doubt about it. Some churches in communities such as Paradise, Texas, may have a more challenging path to reaching more people for Jesus, but the opportunity still exists. In many ways, that challenge (or opportunity, depending on how you look at it) is growing every day. That's why we need more churches to experience the same growth that the church in Acts experienced.

Am I suggesting that if your church is not growing, it isn't healthy? The fact is, I do see instances where healthy churches go through pruning seasons, just like healthy plants. Pruning is not unusual when churches establish a new vision or shift strategies. In the short run, that may cause some people to leave, and the church may then experience a season of decline. If the vision and strategy are from God, though, I'm confident the church will eventually return to growth as more people come to faith and the Lord adds to the fellowship.

In other words, sometimes decline needs to happen before a church can experience increase. That said, I do think you need to step back and look at the trends over time. If your church has plateaued or started to decline, and that trend goes from months to years, shifting from a temporary setback to the norm, it could very well be a sign that your church is not healthy. At the very least, it's an indication you've moved from the left side of the life cycle to the right side. When that happens, something has to change in order for it to return to health.

Establish and Maintain Unity: Be Ruthless About Eliminating Any Division, Particularly at the Leadership Level

This feels as if it should be obvious, but I run into so many instances where division is creating a huge barrier for churches who desire health and ultimately growth. Of course, this should be no surprise. Paul ran into this challenge with the church in Corinth. He had to challenge them to come together and embrace unity: "I appeal to you, dear brothers and sisters, by the authority of our Lord Jesus Christ, to live in harmony with each other. Let there be no divisions in the church. Rather, be of one mind, united in thought and purpose" (1 Cor. 1:10).

We think we have challenges in our churches. The church in Corinth helped set the bar when it comes to dysfunction. They were divided over leadership (1 Cor. 1:12). They were divided over marriage (1 Cor. 7). They were divided over what they consumed (1 Cor. 8). They were divided over the role of women (1 Cor. 11:2–16). They were divided over spiritual gifts (1 Cor. 14). It's apparent that the more things change, the more they stay the same.

With that background, it's no surprise that Paul laid down the law with the church about eliminating division. I think it's interesting that he encouraged the church to be on the same page when it comes to "thought and purpose." That's certainly the foundation for unity. With that, I challenge churches to be united around the following:

- **Doctrine.** Every church should establish a statement of faith that confirms their theological underpinning.
- **Mission.** There should be one sentence defining why the church exists.
- **Vision.** There should be agreement on what the church is planning and praying it will be in the future.
- **Strategy.** Leadership must have agreement on how that vision will be accomplished.
- **Values.** Because values shape the culture, the team must agree on the values they embrace.

In these areas, there should be full alignment, particularly at the leadership level. In other words, there should not be anyone paid to be on the ministry staff who doesn't fully agree with the items I've outlined above. If there's any sense there's not full alignment, that person should not be hired. If that person is already on the team and there's any indication there's not alignment, you need to respond with an immediate conversation and coaching.

Then, if alignment still does not happen, that person needs to be removed from the team.

The same holds true for lay leaders. Whether someone is serving on a board or leading a ministry team, unity should be a requirement for every lay leader. If there's any hint of division with people who have influence over others, that needs to be addressed immediately.

That's the priority, but this principle really applies to everyone in the church. It's always amazing to me how churches take such a hard line on some sins but not others. Creating division in the church is a sin. It should be confronted like every other sin using the principles we see for biblical conflict resolution in Matthew 18:15–20. I've seen too many church leaders shy away from tough conversations because they didn't want to upset the wrong person, only to find that, over time, a cancer had developed in the body of Christ.

This is a big deal. Jesus also confirmed the priority of maintaining unity within the church, such as in his prayer in John 17:21–23:

> I pray that they will all be one, just as you and I are one—as you are in me, Father, and I am in you. And may they be in us so that the world will believe you sent me.
>
> I have given them the glory you gave me, so they may be one as we are one. I am in them and you are in me. May they experience such perfect unity that the world will know that you sent me and that you love them as much as you love me.

Jesus links unity to how people outside the church view us. You, of course, know that's true. When a church is unified and firing on all cylinders to fulfill its mission, the community feels that. They may not want to acknowledge it, but the impact is undeniable.

On the other hand, if division exists in the church, the community knows about that too. Whether we want to admit it or not, there's an undeniable impact on our witness to the world around us if we allow division to take hold.

Now, let me distinguish alignment with healthy conflict. On healthy teams, there should always be healthy conflict. That conflict, though, should be between people who have unity at the foundation. Where that exists, trust will develop that should create freedom for smart, high-capacity leaders to engage in healthy conversations about how to fulfill the vision and strategy. You want aligned team members who are willing to offer new ideas, question practices that are broken, and push back to refine new initiatives. That's a good thing. The last thing you want, on the other hand, is a team of people around you that acquiesces to everything you say. That's not a sign of unity built on trust and loyalty. That's unity forced through fear and cult-like indoctrination.

At the foundation, the church should be unified. When that happens, the power of any team is multiplied. In no other organization is that more true than within the body of Christ. This is God's design for a church that desires sustained health.

Multiply Your Impact: The Mission Is Not About You but Rather Your Need to Mobilize Others

This is one of the definitive marks of a church that's reached sustained health: the ministry is mobilized beyond the walls of the church. What that mobilization leading to multiplication looks like will differ, but the end result is that the footprint of the church's mission expands beyond its current territory. That's when the mission becomes a movement.

The standard, once again, was set by the early church. We see several versions of how the multiplication occurred. As one example, there's a challenge to raise up new teachers and disciple makers. We see that, for instance, in Paul's encouragement to Timothy:

> You have heard me teach things that have been confirmed by many reliable witnesses. Now teach these truths to other trustworthy people who will be able to pass them on to others. (2 Tim. 2:2)

What a great picture of mentoring someone else. Paul didn't hold on to the gospel message for himself. He imparted it to Timothy. But developing Timothy wasn't the win. The win was seeing him disciple others. That's multiplication.

That should challenge you as a church to fully assess your discipleship strategy. Often I see a discipleship path look like the following:

WORSHIP → GROW → SERVE → ENGAGE

These are the steps the church asks its people to take, and then it builds programs around each of those steps. There's a service to attend. There's a Sunday school class or small group to go to. There's a volunteer team to be on. There's a missions or outreach trip to do. These are not bad things, but they rarely lead to mentoring relationships. They push people into adding more activities to their already busy schedule. They feed the consumer mind-set that's pervasive in our culture. And they don't move people to pass the gospel on to others.

Whatever you decide your discipleship path is going to be, the final step should be the challenge Paul gave to Timothy. The path should lead to influencing and leading others. Will everybody take that step? I doubt it, but we should set that bar high.

Similarly, we see a multiplication of leadership in the early church. Again, Paul understood he could not do it on his own. Instead, he raised up other leaders for the church. For example, he wrote, "I left you on the island of Crete so you could complete our work there and appoint elders in each town as I instructed you" (Titus 1:5).

In other words, it's not enough to pass on knowledge and wisdom; we also have to mobilize biblically qualified leaders to extend our reach. Again, this is not a normal practice in churches today. We get so focused on our ministry programming to keep church-goers busy that we lose sight of the fact that we are supposed to be mobilizing people to take new territory. We are not good at raising up leaders, pouring into them, and then encouraging them to take bold steps to multiply the gospel reach.

Nowhere is this challenge to mobilize and multiply more evident than when Jesus calls the church to launch a movement:

> You will receive power when the Holy Spirit comes upon you. And you will be my witnesses, telling people about me every-where—in Jerusalem, throughout Judea, in Samaria, and to the ends of the earth. (Acts 1:8)

Wherever Jerusalem is for your church today, Jesus has called you to eventually go beyond that community as well. Again, that's going to look different for different churches. For some that may be extending the ministries of the church into the community so that gospel transformation happens in people's lives. For other churches that may mean mobilizing and multiplying by opening new campuses of the church through a multisite approach. For others it may mean planting new churches in other parts of the region or the world around us. Whatever the case, God's design is for the church to expand its territory.

Hopefully the priority of everything I've mentioned when talking about the strategic growth season is beginning to make sense now. It's possible to grow one church in one location without having a strategy for multiplication. It's impossible to grow one church in multiple locations—whether that's ministries, campuses, or churches—without having an intentional strategy for multiplication.

That's why churches that sustain health are asking if their growth can be replicated.

You have a strong senior pastor today, but do you have a succession strategy in place for the next senior pastor? Can that be replicated?

You have an incredible team of staff and lay leaders now, but do you have a leadership development strategy to send your best leaders out to launch new works? Can they be replicated?

You have a sense that people are taking their next steps toward Christ, but are you confident that your discipleship strategy is really happening outside of the teaching on Sunday mornings? Can your discipling be replicated?

You're confident you can sustain health in one location, but do you have a multiplication strategy that will work to open a new campus or plant a new church? Can your growth be replicated?

My point is that you can't skip the season of strategic growth, including all the hard work that's required, and assume your ministry will just drift along toward sustained health.

Don't Hold On to the Past: Healthy Churches Embrace New Changes to Get New Results

This isn't about your church, though it may be about your church. This isn't about your leadership, though it may be about your leadership. This isn't about your spiritual journey, though it may be about your spiritual journey. This is a story about me.

I like being comfortable. I like life the way I like life. What's crazy is that God doesn't want me to be comfortable. Instead, he's warned me:

> Don't long for "the good old days."
> This is not wise.
> (Eccl. 7:10)

When it comes down to it, none of us really likes change. Our natural tendency is to drift to that which is comfortable. That's why we tend to get bent out of shape when someone challenges our thinking. Our personal preferences are sacred. But the Lord says:

> Forget the former things;
> do not dwell on the past.
> See, I am doing a new thing!
> Now it springs up; do you not perceive it?
> I am making a way in the wilderness
> and streams in the wasteland.
> (Isa. 43:18–19 NIV)

I like certain songs sung at a certain volume with a certain amount of lighting. I like certain ministries with certain activities that meet on a certain day of the week. I like certain teachings around certain passages that address the sins of certain people (who aren't me).

> Sing a new song to the LORD!
> Let the whole earth sing to the LORD!
> (Ps. 96:1)

New things make me uncomfortable. New things require me to give up control. New things make me change. New things force me to become, in a way, a new person.

> And no one puts new wine into old wineskins. For the wine would burst the wineskins, and the wine and the skins would both be lost. New wine calls for new wineskins. (Mark 2:22)

As a leader, sometimes I have to pursue new methods when I know it's going to disrupt people. It's going to make them uncomfortable. They might not like that. They may not like me. It's just easier to keep things the way they are. I like comfortable, because I want people to like me.

> This means that anyone who belongs to Christ has become a new person. The old life is gone; a new life has begun! (2 Cor. 5:17)

This is what I've learned about myself. I want to have new influence without giving up my old ways. I want to reach new people without giving up my old methods. I want to become a new person without giving up my old life.

We know, of course, that's not possible. The same holds true for churches. Churches can't have new influence without giving up their old ways. They can't reach new people without giving up their old methods. Churches can't see people experience new life in Christ without challenging them to give up their old life.

There's nothing watered down in that challenge, is there?

Churches that sustain health over any length of time get this. They recognize their message will stay the same, but their methods must change.

Without question, one of the factors that drives momentum and health for a church is adaptability. When I mention that, I'll bet your thoughts immediately gravitate to the church that's stood for decades on the corner of First Street and Main in your community. They've been holding the same services and using the same songs and meeting at the same time for the last fifty years. That's not the church I have in mind.

The church I envision is the one that was growing until recently. They found methods that worked for a while, but now they've plateaued or started to decline. They know change is needed, but they're unwilling to change because it might offend the people who already attend the church. People might stop coming. People might stop giving. Everything inside them is fighting to pursue revival so they can return to the health and growth their church was experiencing in the past. But the voices inside the church have become louder than those outside the church.

That's not the mind-set of a church experiencing sustained health. Healthy churches have a willingness to change methods ingrained in their culture. Not every church has this in their DNA. That's part of the reason why not every church is experiencing health.

So when people think church services are boring and irrelevant to their lives, healthy churches adapt and begin to change their worship services to reach new people.

When the ministry environments become packed and impersonal because of growth, healthy churches adapt and begin to offer a path for people to connect in small groups and serving teams.

When the culture shifts and raises the value of serving the hurting and the hopeless, healthy churches adapt and begin to engage their communities with strategies to impact people outside the walls of the church.

When it seems people are less likely to attend services in auditoriums that seat thousands in buildings that become financially less feasible, healthy churches adapt and begin to gather in multiple locations at smaller venues.

Have you ever noticed that some ministries thrive for a while and then begin to decline while others have sustained health and impact decade after decade? One of the reasons is because these healthy churches have made it part of their culture to implement changes and embrace what's new. Healthy churches today are not the same churches they were ten, five, or even two years ago.

Here's what's interesting about change and doing new things. It feels more sacred and more holy to hold on to the way things were. Traditions can be a good thing as long as they don't become barriers to what God wants us to do next.

So ask yourself, is it sacred or is it familiar? Is it holy or is it comfortable?

Sometimes I have to embrace change because God wants to change me.

Be Generous: Stewardship Is a Better
Financial Strategy Than Hope

Ministry is challenging because the win is hard to measure. We want people to experience new life in Christ. But let's face it, people can learn to talk a good talk. Savvy people can say what they think you want to hear.

And it goes beyond words to actions. Sure, actions speak louder than words, but doing lots of churchy things doesn't necessarily mean someone is becoming more like Christ. It's possible to have a vast gulf between doing and becoming.

Even attitudes and emotions can tell a story that's not necessarily true. Some people have learned to fake it until they make it. It's so challenging because we want to know that God is *really* doing a transformative work in their life.

At some point, you want to strip away the words, the actions, and the attitudes and confirm where their heart is.

As hard as it may be to believe, Jesus gave us a way of measuring someone's heart. It actually has nothing to do with words or actions or attitudes. The measure has to do with money. He said, "Wherever your treasure is, there the desires of your heart will also be" (Matt. 6:21).

It's so true, isn't it? I know that to be the case in my life. I can talk about full surrender all I want, but my checkbook and my credit card statement tell the truth. Where my treasure is, there the desires of my heart will also be.

As I mentioned previously, I've always thought Jesus got that principle backward. I've wondered why he didn't say, "Wherever your heart is, there your treasure will also be." It seems like the priority should be getting your heart right first, and then you'll be more generous. But Jesus switched it around. He put money first. It's as if he knew practicing generosity impacts the condition of our heart. It's as if he knew that developing a healthy perspective around stewardship would change us. Could discipline precede transformation?

You've probably preached this message. Or maybe you wanted to preach this message but were afraid to because you've been convinced that people don't want to hear you talk about money. Well, let's forget about people for a moment. Did you know this same principle applies to churches?

Whenever I go into a church, I can tell a lot about the heart of the church based on where their treasure is. Some churches are tight with their money. It's a reflection of their heart. Some churches are open-handed and generous with their money. It's a reflection of their heart.

What may surprise you, though, is how churches tend to become generous. And, again, the principles are a little counterintuitive.

There are generally two types of churches when it comes to how they manage their money. The first group looks at what came in last year and then adds a percentage that it hopes to receive in the coming year. They view that additional percentage as the faith portion of their budget.

Other churches begin in the same place. They first look at what came in last year, but they subtract a percentage from what they expect to receive in the coming year. They argue that the entire budget requires faith.

These are two distinctive approaches to managing money, and they tend to lead to two very different outcomes. Frankly, it all comes down to stewardship. For that reason, I put the first group of churches in the foolish category when it comes to the stewardship of financial resources, and I categorize the second group to be wise in their approach. The following table details the trends that distinguish the two:

	Foolish Trends	Wise Trends
Budgeting	Plan to spend it all plus more than they've received in the past.	Plan to spend less than they expect to receive based on their past.
Tough Choices	Unwilling to cut expenses for long-term financial health.	Routinely prioritize expenses and eliminate anything that's not mission critical.
Culture	Because the "faith" amount rarely comes in, the church is constantly in budget reduction mode. Budget freezes are common.	Because the church often receives more than it plans to spend, it's routinely in budget increase mode. It's an opportunity to make new investments.
Generosity	Typically stingy with their investments outside the ministry because money is always tight.	Typically very generous with their investments outside the ministry because money is always available
New Initiatives	Always trying to fund what they've done in the past.	Always looking for new opportunities to grow the kingdom.
Finance Team	Give freedom during the budgeting process and tighten the reins throughout the ministry year.	Tighten the reins during the budgeting process creating freedom throughout the ministry year.

I want churches to be wiser with their financial resources because it creates opportunities for generosity, including investments in new kingdom initiatives that the foolish will never be able to afford.

Which direction does your church lean? These questions might help you diagnose your tendency:

- Do you plan to spend less than you reasonably expect to receive?
- Are you willing to make some tough calls and cut

expenditures in some areas to fund other ministry priorities?

- Have you found yourself in the enviable position of finding new ways to bless others or expand your vision because you received more than you planned to spend?
- Are you fully funding your growth engines, both numerical and spiritual, to experience new kingdom impact rather than just funding what you've done in the past?
- Does your budgeting process create freedom for ministry leaders to accomplish the mission that God's placed on your church?

If you answered no to any of these questions, it may be time to revisit whether or not you are wisely stewarding your financial resources.

In any case, what this approach to wise stewardship offers is a basis for churches to sustain health. It challenges churches to live within their means. As that happens, it increases the opportunities for the church to be generous with its community, to fund vision expansion, to multiply and take new territory, and to financially take care of the people who the church is paying to help lead the ministry.

I love the apostle Paul's reminder about the importance of generosity:

Remember this—a farmer who plants only a few seeds will get a small crop. But the one who plants generously will get a generous crop. You must each decide in your heart how much to give. And don't give reluctantly or in response to pressure. "For God loves a person who gives cheerfully." And God will generously provide all you need. Then you will always have everything you need and plenty left over to share with others. (2 Cor. 9:6–8)

My hope is that you will experience what it's like to have plenty left over to share with others. It begins with becoming a good steward of the money God has given us to manage.

I'm praying for more and more churches to experience the sustained health I've described in this chapter. Churches in this phase of the life cycle are making new disciples, pursuing continued growth, maintaining unity, multiplying their impact, embracing change, and being generous. I hope you'll join me in praying for more churches to experience sustained health. Imagine the life change and community impact we would see if more churches were ministering at this level of health.

Part of me wishes this was the end of the book, but not all churches will remain in sustained health. Most will at some point or another move further along on the life cycle to a season of maintenance. Let's unpack the characteristics of churches that have moved into maintenance mode and discover the strategies that could help them return to sustained health.

CHAPTER 5

MAINTENANCE

It's Time to Embrace a New Vision All Over Again

Don't you just want to stop reading right now? Until this point in our journey, everything was up and to the right. We were experiencing momentum and growth and health, and then, all of a sudden, we find ourselves on the other side of the life cycle. It snuck up on us, didn't it?

Only it's never "all of a sudden." The shift, short of a crisis of some sort, never happens in an instant. Frankly, even a crisis moment shouldn't cause a shift to the right side of the life cycle for healthy churches. In fact, I've seen many healthy churches face the challenges of a local natural disaster, economic downturn, leadership transition, or even a moral failure and emerge stronger than they were before. The root of the shift to this maintenance phase goes much deeper than that.

Because of that, churches are typically in the maintenance season for months or even years before they realize it. That's what's so challenging about the three phases on the right side of the life cycle. They are hard to confirm and even harder to accept. Many times churches are well established in one of these seasons of decline before any awareness sets in.

Compounding this challenge is the fact that leaders will certainly identify it before the congregation does. Leaders tend to understand the present condition and future ramifications before others. That's a characteristic of those who really have the spiritual gift of leadership and those who do not. Because of that, leaders learn to help others understand the consequences looming in the present reality so they're in a strong position to cast vision and increase urgency to embrace a better future. That's one of the keys to leading change.

In no season is the assessment of the condition of the church more confusing than during this maintenance phase. One of the reasons is that it can feel like the strategic growth phase in so many ways. The differences are very subtle. For example, churches moving up the life cycle in the strategic growth season and those declining in the maintenance season share these common characteristics:

- Both typically have an established mission, vision, and strategy for the future.
- Both have strong leaders at both the staff and lay leadership level.
- Both have strong giving. In fact, as I'll explain in the coming pages, it's not uncommon for churches to experience the strongest giving ever in this maintenance season.
- Both types of churches have new people connecting to the church and are seeing people become new believers.
- Both have implemented systems and processes to support their ministry strategy.

Both types of churches can look healthy on the surface, and yet, when you dig a little deeper, you will find a combination of factors to confirm that one is moving toward sustained health and the other has started to decline.

This is where the size of the church certainly has nothing to do with where it might be on the life cycle. There are some very large churches in the maintenance phase. Some know it, and some do not. What's challenging is that some of those large churches don't realize they've started down the path on the right side of the life cycle, but they're still blogging, podcasting, and conferencing like nothing has changed. They're not doing that on purpose. They just don't realize they've moved into a maintenance season, and their drive to help resource other churches hasn't paused.

I'm all for churches sharing what's working and not working in their ministries. That sharpens all of us. We should be open-handed with what we're learning, particularly in the church. After all, we share the same ultimate mission. It just means we also need to be more diligent and discerning to determine whether or not the church is sharing from current or past health.

Earlier this week, one of my daughters was not feeling well. Her symptoms dragged on for a couple of days, and she wasn't getting better. We decided to take her to a clinic to determine what was wrong. The doctor administered a test and completed an exam to confirm it was just a virus. She gave some coaching to help our daughter deal with the symptoms, but there was no medicine to treat the illness. It would just take time for her to feel better.

I wish diagnosing the health of a church was as easy as that. Wouldn't it be nice if you could take a quick test and determine whether or not a dose of medicine or some other treatment plan was needed? That would help, but it's not possible.

What I can help you with are some common characteristics I've found in churches that have shifted into this maintenance phase. As I said in the previous chapter, any one attribute on its own may not provide a confirmation that attention is needed. A combination of these, though, might very well help you determine that it's time to treat the patient.

1. *Attendance growth plateaus or begins to decline.* It's not all about attendance, but attendance is certainly a factor when assessing health. Every church experiences the ups and downs of attendance patterns. One indicator of a church in the maintenance phase, though, is that these plateaus or dips extend from months to years.

2. *The church becomes insider-focused.* The voices of people inside the church become louder than those of people outside the church and outside the faith. When this happens, attendance numbers, group connections, event participation, serving, and other indicators of health may stay strong, but the number of salvations and baptisms starts to decline.

3. *The vision stales.* There's still a vision. In fact, it might be painted on the wall in the lobby of the church. The problem is, that vision fades over time. It has to be renewed. Some churches in this maintenance season have a vision, but it's too generic. It's not specific and measurable. In other instances, there's an established mission and vision, but the systems and methods have become more important. The *how* becomes a higher priority than the *why*.

4. *Ministry silos begin to form.* Rather than one team pulling in one direction, ministries begin to prioritize their programming over the health of the overall church. The children's department is only focused on kid's programming. The education department is only focused

on Bible studies and classes. The men's ministry is only focused on men's programming. Before you know it, the church has become program-driven. There are lots of new programs and new events, but they're pulling people in different directions and creating complexity.

5. *The church becomes overstaffed.* On the way up the life cycle, more and more resources became available to hire more people any time a new challenge popped up. Rather than raising up volunteers to engage the ministry, more of the ministry shifted to staff. Compounding this issue is the fact that most of that hiring happened from the inside (people already attending the church). Without fresh perspectives from the outside, staff teams tend to do the same thing they've always done and hope for different results.

6. *They remain financially healthy.* Sounds counterintuitive, doesn't it? When a church is experiencing growth and health on the left side of the life cycle, there are more unbelievers and new believers in the church. They typically don't give. That's why growing churches are stretched financially. Mature churches have a higher percentage of Christ followers who have matured in their faith, including their generosity and obedience about giving. That's why it's not uncommon for a church in the maintenance phase to be financially healthier than a church experiencing strategic growth on the opposite side of the cycle.

Here's the good news. Unlike my daughter's virus, there's a treatment for churches in this maintenance season. They don't have to stay here. They don't all continue down the life cycle toward death. They can return to sustained health. The challenge, though, is that the treatment isn't easy. Let me unpack some of the next steps that are needed to help these churches experience health again.

Renew the Vision: Embrace the Change Before the Emergency Forces the Change

I've noticed that sometimes leaders get confused about mission and vision. They're not the same thing. The mission explains why an organization exists; the vision clarifies where the organization is going in the future. The mission is a short statement that's typically twelve words or less. The vision, when written down, will be longer in order to map out where the organization will be in the years to come. When developing vision, I like to look three to five years into the future.

Because of this confusion, I've seen church leaders develop "vision statements" that are really mission statements. I've also seen churches hold on to those pseudovision statements for way too long. That's particularly challenging, because one-sentence statements, though they can confirm the purpose of a church's existence, typically can't provide a lot of specifics about where the church hopes to be down the road. Without specifics, you can't paint the picture of the future. Without that clear picture, it's impossible to rally people to the cause.

That's why it's important to remember that the mission of an organization will rarely, if ever, change. The vision, on the other hand, needs to be refreshed every few years or so.

For a church that has plateaued and started down the right side of the life cycle, this is a critical first step to return to health.

Unfortunately, as I alluded to in the overview of the maintenance phase of the life cycle, sometimes churches don't even recognize they've started to decline. As I work with church leaders, I've noticed that it's difficult for those inside a ministry to discern where they are in their own life cycle. Many times they don't realize it, but the pinnacle of health, growth, and impact is in the rearview mirror.

For example, I worked with a church that, for a couple of decades, rode the wave to sustained health. They were planted out of a mainline denomination, but everything about the church was fresh and dynamic. Their doctrine was the same as their peer churches, but the methods of engaging ministry were very different.

For more than twenty years the church grew and eventually reached thousands of people—many who found faith in Christ through the church's ministry. In the final years of growth, though, the vision became stale. They continued to proceed forward as they had the previous two decades, but without a fresh infusion of vision and strategy, the church, though still relatively young, began to hold on to its past. A passion for reaching people outside the faith began to shift to ministries for people who were already attending the church. A church that was founded with change ingrained in its culture began to dig in and embrace their new traditions. The ministry that once had a fresh, big vision was instead operating on vision fumes. There were still thousands of people showing up every weekend, but years before they realized it, the church had started to decline.

When I think about that church, I'm reminded that a distinctive style of worship is not a vision. That's part of a strategy to accomplish a vision. Eventually that distinctive style will become predictable and expected. Other churches will duplicate it. It will become common.

Building a new facility isn't a vision either. It can be part of the vision, but eventually the building project will be completed. If that's the extent of the vision, people will assume you've arrived and the vision has been attained when the building is finished.

Also, as I think about that once-vibrant church that became stuck, it's a reminder that numbers aren't the problem, but they can cloud the issue. For example, I've worked with several churches that are still growing, but their best years are behind them. It's residual growth. They're still riding the last waves of a once-fresh vision and strategy. Because they are still growing, they don't realize there's a problem right in front of them.

The church's financial position can compound the challenge. In the early phases of the life cycle, particularly during the launch and momentum growth phases, it's not unusual for many people outside the faith and brand-new believers to be engaged in the ministry. It's great having these fresh faces connected to the life of the church, but for obvious reasons, they don't financially contribute to the ministry like mature Christ followers do. During this time, it's quite common for attendance growth to exceed giving growth. This creates a giving lag, because it takes time for new believers to start making financial contributions to the church's vision.

As the new believers become fully devoted followers of Christ, financial growth begins to catch up with numerical growth. This allows churches to increase their investment in staff, ministry programming, and facilities, among other things. And with that, new patterns and habits form.

One example is that churches tend to hold on to the ministry programs and strategies that originally produced health and growth. It's ironic, because churches in the launch and momentum growth seasons typically embrace change. That's part of why they experience success. Over time, though, habits start to take root. Once a necessity, change is now an inconvenience. As necessary changes become obvious, many churches simply avoid the warning signs and don't make any changes until they feel the pain.

The challenge is that churches often feel safe because money hasn't stopped coming in even as attendance has slowed or declined. In fact, per-capita giving can actually be the highest when a church is in decline. This picture demonstrates how the giving lag comes into play both as attendance increases and then declines:

One of the obvious reasons why a church starts to decline is because there are fewer new people. In other words, there aren't as many people who are still considering the claims of Jesus and there are fewer new believers. As the church matures, there is often a higher percentage of people who are mature in their faith. Because of this dynamic, attendance may be in decline, but giving is still very strong. That's because the giving lag is working in reverse from how it operated during the early days.

The Giving Lag

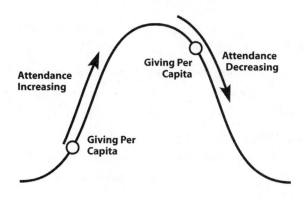

Since giving is still strong, it's not unusual for churches to live in denial. There's no pain. They can sustain the staff. They can retain all their ministry programming. They can hold on to a tired vision and strategy. Since there isn't any financial pain, there's no urgency to change. Of course, if you want to return to health and avoid the next two stages of the life cycle, you're going to have to change before the emergency occurs.

The place to begin this change is with the vision. The vision needs to be refreshed. There needs to be a clear picture, once again, of where the church is going in the future. I won't replay what a healthy vision looks like here, because I covered that in the momentum growth phase. But let me offer these suggestions for how you might go about renewing the vision:

- Don't go at it alone. Involve a dozen or so strategically minded leaders in the process. You will benefit from a collaborative process.
- Don't try to develop a vision with the entire congregation having a voice. You can't survey your way to vision. God's leaders should develop the vision for God's church. You'll never get consensus for the future if everyone has a voice in the future.
- Once you have the building blocks of the vision in place, engage other leaders, both staff and lay leaders, in developing the action plan. In other words, a small group of leaders should shape the vision, and then a larger group of leaders should put the strategy in motion to help the vision become reality.
- Communicate the new vision with the key stakeholders first. Begin with the staff and leadership boards. Share

it with your volunteer leaders before you communicate it to the entire congregation. When you cast the vision, you'll need to start by explaining why staying where you are will be more painful than making the necessary changes to move forward.

- Use the renewed vision as an opportunity to rally people with their prayers, their time, and their financial resources. Give people a chance to join the cause.
- Don't be surprised when a renewed vision causes some people to leave the church. Any big, bold vision for the future will certainly turn some people away. Every great vision experiences this. Yours will not be the exception.

It's essential that churches try to begin a new life cycle if they find themselves in this maintenance phase. Before you begin making any other changes, though, you must begin by developing a fresh vision. The mission and this renewed vision will drive all the necessary changes that will follow.

Prioritize Reaching New People: Reconfirm the Primary Person You're Trying to Reach Who Is Outside the Church

If I had to identify only one key factor distinguishing churches on the left side of the life cycle and those on the right side, it would be this one. Churches that are moving up the life cycle toward sustained health maintain a focus on reaching people outside the faith and outside the church. On the other hand, churches that are plateaued or declining and moving down the right side of the life cycle have begun to turn inward. The farther down the life cycle they go, the more inward-focused they are.

The key question that leaders need to address is, what are we willing to do to reach people outside the church and outside the faith? The churches on the upswing will do just about anything short of sin to reach new people. If what they're doing today doesn't accomplish that goal, they'll embrace changes as they move forward toward accomplishing that goal. For churches on the downside of the life cycle, they're not inclined to make any changes to reach new people if it means losing people who already attend the church.

That means there are generally two types of churches: outward-focused churches and inward-focused churches. Both face distinctive challenges and both have strategic opportunities to move toward sustained health.

For the outward-focused church, the primary challenge will be how we help people take steps in their spiritual journeys after they accept Christ. In other words, outward-focused churches, by their nature, are more adept at creating environments where the unchurched or dechurched are welcomed. They are typically more evangelistic in their approach, but they have to work at discipleship.

What I've learned, though, is that most outward-focused churches are very sensitive to this challenge. These leaders are uncomfortable with people getting stuck spiritually. That may actually be a reflection of their evangelistic bent, because they recognize that people with vibrant relationships with Jesus want to continue to reach people outside the faith. Their goal is to get maturing Christians engaged in the mission.

The inward-focused church has a different challenge, however. Their primary barrier to health is creating environments designed to reach people who don't have a relationship with Jesus. Inward-focused churches typically design their environments primarily with discipleship in mind. Unfortunately, I find that most inward-focused churches are not sensitive to the barriers they've created for reaching the people who are still considering the claims of Christ and/or are not connected in a church.

In these instances, leaders are uncomfortable with any changes that might address that challenge for fear that it might push insiders away and, frankly, impact the bottom line. Ironically, any organization, including a church, that doesn't focus on reaching new people has already started to decline and will eventually die.

This may be hard for you to digest, but I've seen most (though not all) outward-focused churches have a very intentional path for spiritual development. Many offer discipleship opportunities to help people take steps toward Christ outside of the weekend service. And of the churches I've worked with, most of the students and adults who attend those churches are engaged in that discipleship path.

On the other hand, inward-focused churches rarely have anything intentional for reaching people outside the faith. If anything, they try to create evangelism programs rather than fully engage a strategy, particularly using their weekend services, to reach the unchurched or dechurched. In those instances, inward-focused churches hope (and sometimes pray) that people outside the faith will somehow join what the church is already doing for existing church members. When it comes to reaching people outside the faith, I've never seen that strategy work.

For example, I worked with a church a few years ago that had started to decline in attendance and baptisms. In their minds, the solution was to develop an evangelism training program for all the church members. They thought the problem would be fixed with more knowledge. If those members could be trained on one-on-one evangelism, more people would accept Christ and connect with the church.

What that church failed to address was the fact that their Sunday services were completely insider-focused and their Sunday school classes were competing with their children's ministry for both leaders and facility space. They were investing their best leadership and space in older generations. There's nothing necessarily wrong with that other than that it was competing with their desire to see new, young families connect with the church. Instead of dealing with the core issues of reshaping their worship services and Sunday school program, they chose the easy option, which was to offer an evangelism training program. That effort didn't work.

In case you're curious, here are some common symptoms I see in churches that are inward-focused:

- **The bulletin is loaded with announcements.** Usually this is an indication the church is focused on programs rather than people. Programs are competing for people's attention rather than creating a clear path for new people to take the next steps.
- **There are lots of meetings.** The more inwardly-focused a church gets, the more board and committee meetings there are to talk about buildings and budgets. When people are on a mission to reach others, there are fewer meetings.
- **You don't hear and share stories of life change.** Instead, you're more likely to hear about all the activities happening in the church.

- **There's only one Sunday service.** Inwardly-focused churches are more concerned about knowing and seeing everyone. That becomes the higher value over reaching new people.
- **If there is more than one service, there are multiple styles of worship.** There's a traditional service, a blended service, and a contemporary service. That's an indication the worship is more about the preferences of people who already attend the church.
- **Change of any sort is resisted.** It doesn't matter how big or small the change. Service times. Paint color. Room assignments. Service order. Song selection. Inwardly-focused churches are more interested in preserving the past.
- **People are not inviting their friends.** Because of that, the gut reaction may be to teach more on evangelism, but that typically doesn't fix the problem. Instead, the services and ministries need to be designed to reach people outside the church. When we intentionally create environments where life change happens, people want to attend and invite their friends.

Jason Fried and David Heinemeier Hansson wrote a book titled *Rework* that has nothing to do with ministry, and yet this statement has everything to do with ministry: "When you stick with your current customers come hell or high water, you wind up cutting yourself off from new ones. Your product or service becomes so tailored to your current customers that it stops appealing to fresh blood. And that's how your company starts to die."[1]

If we restated this thought for our purposes, it would read as follows: When everything you do is focused on people who already attend your church, you create barriers for engaging new people. And that's how your church starts to die.

Jesus explained it this way: "If a man has a hundred sheep and one of them gets lost, what will he do? Won't he leave the ninety-nine others in the wilderness and go to search for the one that is lost until he finds it?" (Luke 15:4).

That's a big challenge for us as we tend to think about the ninety-nine, because their voices are always going to be louder than the one.

Curtail the Complexity Creep: Shift from Adding Programs to Clarifying a Path

As our team at The Unstuck Group engages with the churches we serve, we always begin by completing an assessment to understand the current health of the ministry. Through that process, we try to narrow down the core issues that are holding the church back from experiencing health and growth. Those are the issues we help the church address through the strategic planning process.

With very few exceptions, the vast majority of churches I've served have concluded that they are too complex. For some, the complexity has more to do with their governance and how decisions are made. That's a challenge we'll hit in the next phase of the life cycle. The more common form of complexity I see, though, has to do with ministry programming. Churches freely admit they're overprogrammed. They know they're trying to do too much.

Since the research is clear that more church activity does not produce spiritual growth,[2] you would think churches would be inclined to tackle this challenge and eliminate competing programs. The problem, though, is that this complexity develops over time, and it's hard to rein in. It begins with the challenge that exists when many churches don't have a strategy; they have mission statements. They know why they exist. They have a vision. They know where they believe God has called their ministries to be in the future. What they don't have is a strategy on how to accomplish that vision. Without a clearly defined strategy, churches gravitate toward what they've always done, but they add new programs to try to accomplish the new vision. With every iteration of the vision, more things are added, but nothing is ever subtracted. The complexity creep begins.

Then, as we covered in the previous section, churches tend to become insider-focused over time. This isn't just a problem for so-called traditional churches; this is an issue for every church that has existed for any length of time. Unless you work to prevent it, eventually the people inside the church become a higher priority than those outside the church. For fear of making insiders unhappy, churches tend to hold on to ministry programs, even if those programs are not producing health and reaching more people. The complexity creep grows.

Soon churches discover it's easier to add a program than it is to redefine its strategy. For example, churches that are reaching many young adults aren't doing so through a young adults program. They aren't hiring a young adults director and starting a separate young adults gathering. Instead, they're reaching a lot of young adults because their strategy—their weekend services, small groups, serving opportunities, family ministries, and everything in between—is done with young adults in mind. To take that approach, you have to define who you are trying to reach, and your whole strategy needs to reflect that focus. That takes work. It will require change. It may offend some churchgoers. That's why churches take the easy way out and just launch new programs. The complexity creep takes over.

To combat the complexity creep, you need a unified ministry strategy so everyone begins to pull in the same direction. That helps to prioritize how to use space, invest money, leverage leaders, engage volunteers, and promote the next steps. Instead of every ministry protecting its programs and events, the church decides which programs and events are most needed to effectively fulfill its strategy. In other words, the church shifts from a complex matrix of competing programs to a unified discipleship strategy that helps people engage on a spiritual formation path.

Back in the chapter on strategic growth, I talked about the priority of establishing a clear discipleship strategy. I can confirm that the churches experiencing the healthiest growth tend to have a discipleship approach in the form of a path. By that I mean they encourage people in their journey of following Christ by offering a series of clear next steps.

On the other hand, many of the churches I've seen in decline and in this maintenance phase of the life cycle take a distinctly different approach. They rely on an ever-growing collection of programs as the basis for their discipleship strategy. These churches have an overwhelming number of programs for attendees and even the community, but they lack any cohesive path that helps people learn what steps to take and when. I've used a picture like the first figure on the next page to describe the difference.

As you might imagine, there are several key differences between churches with discipleship strategies built around programs and churches with strategies built around a path. The table on the bottom of the next page helps to clarify those differences.

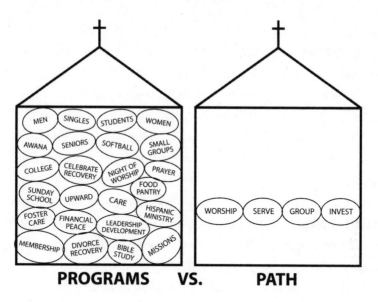

PROGRAMS VS. PATH

Here's the reality: every individual is accountable for their own spiritual growth. And when we look back at our lives, most of the time, it was our relationships that helped us grow in our love for Jesus and our desire to follow him.

Distinctives	Programs	Path
What's the win?	Getting more people involved in activities.	Helping more people take a next step.
What gets communicated?	Everything. There's a competition for getting people's attention.	One thing. The focus is on helping people take one next step.
How is the church structured?	The structure is built around the programs, which leads to teams operating in solos.	The structure is built around the path with teams working together to encourage movement.
How does it impact volunteer engagement?	More programs mean more demand for volunteers, and many times teams are operating out of a volunteer deficit.	More focus means there's less competition for volunteers and more freedom to serve based on their wiring.
What gets prioritized?	Whatever gets on the calendar first.	Whatever helps people move forward on the path.

The advantage of having a simple, clear discipleship path over an assortment of programs is that you make it easy for new followers of Jesus to build important relationships at the right times in their journey. You give them space to ask questions and opportunities to exercise their faith. You also make it simpler for church leaders and the lead volunteers to keep people from falling through the cracks, especially early on, when they need the most guidance and time investment.

All that to say, your path—or your programs—are not going to guarantee spiritual maturity. Making disciples is never going to be a tidy process. The Holy Spirit's work can't be replaced with a class or a method. A discipleship path, however, will help your church serve people better than a bunch of programs. And as we're seeing, there's at least a correlation between a clear path and sustained health.

One more thing: defining a discipleship path without cutting programs won't work. By necessity, the path will be clear when it's the thing you communicate most often and loudest. Keeping all those programs and then trying to communicate your path will only be adding to the noise.

Stop Low-Impact Programs and Events: Reprioritize Resources Around New Initiatives to Accomplish Your Renewed Vision

I'm working with the assumption that if your church is plateaued or declining, something has to change. You can't do the same thing and expect different results. If you are in this maintenance phase, it begins with a renewed vision to reach new people. For that to happen, it's going to take resources. That will include leadership, volunteers, communications focus, space, and money. It's possible you are part of the very first church I've encountered that has extra resources sitting around to invest in a renewed vision. If so, you don't need what I'm about to share. If you're like most churches, though, you're going to have to stop some things to start something new. You will need to reprioritize your limited resources.

Be forewarned: there's nothing easy about what I'm going to offer. Transitioning a church into a different direction with a renewed vision takes courage and perseverance. A church is more likely to succeed if there's established trust, particularly with your key lay leaders, to chart a new course. There must also be a sense of urgency that things can't stay the same. There must be some identifiable pain that causes the church to want to move to a new place.

This sense of urgency is really what distinguishes the churches that are in an early stage of decline and those that are looking at death and ready to shut down. By that I mean churches that are near death typically have more urgency. They're in survival mode. For churches that are closer to the top of the life cycle, urgency can be hard to muster when, at least from outside appearances, the church may be quite successful. People may still be showing up for worship. People may still be accepting Christ and getting baptized. People may still be maturing in their faith. People may still be giving.

As I shared earlier, though, leaders are the first to identify when a pattern of decline has taken root. When that happens, you need to help people understand the urgency before they'll be receptive to anything involving change. There may not be a financial crisis yet, but if your church isn't reaching as many new people and isn't seeing the spiritual transformation and life change you saw in the past, hopefully that spiritual crisis will be louder. Any great leader will take responsibility for making sure that crisis is understood before they engage any of the strategies I'm going to share next.

For those of you who recognize the need to stop some programs and events in order to refocus resources, let me offer a process to determine what to stop. Here's a diagram to help you visualize what I'm about to describe:

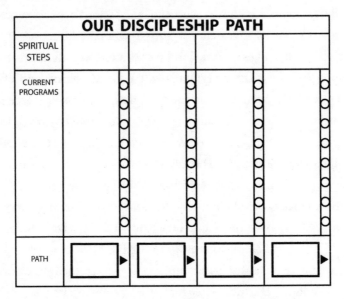

First, begin with your discipleship path. Decide the steps in that path that you want everyone to take. For example, let's assume you create a discipleship path that includes worship, serving, community, and impact. Once you've identified the steps, then list all your ministry programs and events under each of the steps. If a program overlaps steps, then pick the primary spiritual step. If you happen to have any programs or events that don't fit any steps, these will begin your list of things you should stop doing. The reality is that most churches will not have many, if any, programs or events that don't fit somewhere under each of the steps in the discipleship path.

Once you've compiled the lists under each step, then evaluate the health of each of the programs and events. We use green, yellow, and red marks to identify the health of each program. Green represents those programs and events where a higher percentage of people are involved and there's a lot of life change happening. Red is used to label ministries with low engagement and little life change. Yellow is in the middle. You need to come to consensus as a team as you evaluate the health of each of these programs and events.

After you go through the evaluation process, determine the one program or event under each step that you think will effectively lead the most people in their spiritual growth. It'll likely be one of the programs or events you evaluated as green and healthy. You now should have a discipleship path mapped out with a priority next step, either a ministry program or an event, to encourage movement along the path.

Now, with the remaining list, place every item in one of the three categories: (1) red—stop, (2) yellow—pause and reevaluate at a future date, and (3) green—pause and relaunch. You will, of course, want to use the green category sparingly, but there's certainly a place for refreshing and relaunching programs and events if they will eventually help more people engage in the discipleship process.

A pause can be very helpful for gaining perspective. Take a break rather than cancel something altogether. Whether it's a Sunday evening service, the midweek program, or the annual outreach event, just push the pause button. Take a break to test-drive a new solution. You don't have to commit to canceling it forever until people have an opportunity to see what a better future looks like. You may find that the previous solution was actually the better solution.

Once you've determined what you're going to stop doing, then engage an intentional transition process that takes advantage of the following elements.

Give the Stopped Programs an Appropriate Funeral and Burial

Just as you celebrate the life of someone who has gone on to heaven, take the time to celebrate the ministry program or events that you're ending. Tell stories. Acknowledge the contributions of those who have been involved. Give honor where honor is due. And then use that celebration as an opportunity to invite people into the next leg of the journey.

You'll need to engage the key stakeholders early in this process. Who are the leaders and influencers most impacted by the change? Present the challenge to them early so that they can be involved in developing and then owning the solutions as well. Get their buy-in so they can help champion the transition.

To do this effectively, you'll need to communicate openly, honestly, and with kindness. The communications need to be sequenced with the right people at the right time. You have to frequently communicate *why* you're making the change. Begin with one-on-one conversations before meeting with groups. Give individuals opportunities to identify the key questions that need to be addressed, and allow them to speak to the solutions. Ask them who is going to be most impacted by the change, and then talk with those individuals too.

Connect the Change to the Overall Mission and Vision

Of course, this begins with the assumption that you have a clear mission (Why do you exist?) and vision (Where are you headed?). It's much easier to stop a ministry or event if you can point to why resources need to be reinvested to help you fulfill your preferred future.

This is when you'll cast the vision for what's going to be different moving forward. As you do this, consider the underlying value behind the ministry or event you are stopping. It's possible that the value is still important to the ministry; it just needs to be revived with a new strategy or initiative. As you talk about what's changing, define clear expectations for measuring success before the new ministry starts. When everyone is clear on what the win looks like from the beginning, it helps to remove the emotional impact of ending a ministry that may have been successful in the past.

Don't Delay Before or After Initiating the Change

The sooner you can move on the better. Don't let the change process drag on too long. The longer it goes, the more opportunity there will be for negative voices to coalesce around developing a strategy to keep things the way they are.

Don't be surprised if you have to have some tough conversations during the transition. Make sure the leadership is united. This is a biblical command. "Live in harmony with each other. Let there be no divisions in the church. Rather, be of one mind, united in thought and purpose" (1 Cor. 1:10). Fortunately, it's possible to disagree privately on execution and still be fully unified publicly behind mission, vision, and values.

Finally, remember that leading through transitions like this can't be delegated. The senior or lead pastor must lead the change process. The senior pastor must be the primary leader every time significant change is involved. It might help to remind yourself that this is a stewardship matter. Ask yourself: What's the best stewardship of God's resources? With limited money, volunteers, space, communications focus, leadership, staff, etc., what's the wisest investment to see the most life change? Hopefully that reminder will help you stay focused on the right next steps, even if they're challenging.

Believe me, I understand. Change, even the healthiest of changes, is difficult for anyone who is on the receiving end. Keep your focus on the bigger picture. Will more people be reached in the end? If so, take courage and act.

Get a Fresh Perspective: Invest in Outside Help to Disrupt the Inside Voices

Many years ago, when Emily and I were living in Iowa, I was driving down a gravel country road. Emily was in the passenger seat, and Kayla, our only child at the time, was in a car seat in the back. She was probably two at the time.

We had just wrapped up a small group gathering with friends, and we were heading home. It was dusk, and there really wasn't much around us except acres and acres of rolling farmland.

But what started as a pleasant drive through the Iowa countryside suddenly turned into an adventure. An animal jumped out from the other side of the road, struck our windshield, and then landed on the right side of the road. The windshield shattered on impact, but fortunately none of us was hurt. The animal was dazed, lying on the shoulder of the road, but a few minutes later rose to its feet and took off, seemingly unfazed by the incident.

Needless to say, Emily and I were shaken. Meanwhile, Kayla was processing what had just happened. She was trying to put the pieces together and then asked, "Why did that kangaroo jump on our car?"

Now, before you book your next vacation to the Land Down

Under to see the kangaroos jumping around the Iowa cornfields, you may want to consider a few things when it comes to perspective.

First, there are times when we are too close to the problem to see what has actually hit us. We may need to put some time and distance between us and the immediate challenge before we can properly evaluate the problem we're facing. The fog of war can lead to uncertainty. Our judgment can be clouded. That's why we periodically need to retreat and remove ourselves from the battle in order to gain clarity and plan our next steps.

This is important for all church leadership teams, but particularly for those churches in the maintenance season of the life cycle. Whether they realize it or not, they are in a rut, and it's going to take fresh perspective to get out of that rut. There is never an easy time to do this, but you have to make time to pull out of your day-to-day routine and create some space for revisiting the big picture. Why do we exist? Where are we going? How are we going to get there? Who will do it?

Second, our preconceived notions can make it difficult for us to see the truth. In Kayla's experience, the only jumping animals are kangaroos. When an animal jumped on our car, she concluded it was a kangaroo. It's a form of confirmation bias when we see reality through the lens of our existing expectations. That's why it's important to seek outside counsel to help us look at our circumstances from a different perspective.

That's what The Unstuck Group does for the organizations we serve. We bring an unbiased, fresh perspective. We help facilitate the conversations to move from where you are to where God wants your church to be. We don't tell you what to do, but we ask questions and provide a framework for discussion that helps you break out of your current patterns.

I believe in outside facilitation so much that I spend good money every year to bring in outside counsel to support our team. I've learned that it's impossible for me to facilitate strategic planning and engage in the process at the same time. We have others on our team who can facilitate. They're trained. They're experienced. I still spend the extra money to bring a fresh, outside perspective to help guide our conversations, help us find consensus, and then challenge us to put a plan into action.

This is a team effort. Our collective wisdom will generate better wisdom. People will bring unique perspectives. Each has distinct experiences, gifts, and personalities to approach challenges and opportunities. It's another example of how the team outperforms the individual every time. We need one another, especially when we're trying to overcome challenges and take new ground.

I learned long ago that my abilities to develop a vision for the future and the strategy to accomplish that plan are very limited. I can't do it on my own. I've never had that Moses moment when God gave me a plan etched in stone tablets to reveal to the team. I trust that those moments happen for some leaders, but I've found them to be very rare. Instead, I've learned there's strength in engaging a team of people in this process. The right team brings unique experiences, talents, and perspectives. That collaborative approach can be very powerful.

Finally, when it comes to perspective, experience counts. It's probably overstating the obvious, but the perspectives of a two-year-old and that of someone twenty-plus years her senior are quite different. This is one instance when someone with a different perspective has the advantage. Someone looking at the situation with a different filter helps us better understand and interact with the world we see around us.

This is an example of where a strategy that worked during the early stages of the life cycle can actually create problems on the other side. It's not atypical for churches during the momentum and strategic growth stages to do a lot of hiring from within the church. That's a good thing, because you know you're hiring people who are connected with the mission and vision of the church. They know you. You know them.

But if you hire only from inside the church, you only have people who know your perspective. They know your strategy. That's a good thing when the church is moving up the life cycle toward sustained health; that's a problem when you are moving down the life cycle and you need fresh perspective. That's why one symptom of a stuck church is that they haven't hired anyone from the outside. Insiders are strong when it comes to taking proven strategies and systems and executing them. Insiders aren't typically very strong, though, when it comes to making a shift in strategy, systems, or culture. You will likely need some outside hires to make those changes. You need to invest in new leaders with a new perspective to experience new results.

The maintenance season of the life cycle can sneak up on you in many ways. When you identify that you've entered this phase, it's important to establish an intentional plan for returning to health by renewing the vision, reaching new people, eliminating complexity, ending low-impact ministry programs, and getting a fresh perspective. The objective is to try to launch a new life cycle before you slip into the preservation phase.

And one more thing: if you're ever driving down a country road in Iowa, enjoy the journey but watch out for kangaroos.

CHAPTER 6

PRESERVATION

The Church Must Change to Survive

I was sitting at a restaurant across the table from a pastor and listening to him share his story and that of the church he leads. He was still optimistic, so I was trying to guide him in as positive a way as I could. He's leading a church that has several hundred people who attend worship services every Sunday, but the church is in decline. It's been in a slow decline for years. Fewer people are attending, even though the community around the church is growing. Fewer people are accepting Christ and getting baptized. The church is facing a financial crunch because giving is down. The congregation is aging and no longer reflects the community around the church.

Somewhere along the way, the church shifted from maintenance to preservation. I'm sure their intent wasn't to facilitate the decline in the church. They didn't set out to shift from being a vibrant ministry that was experiencing health and growth to a ministry that's focused on preserving the past. Unfortunately, though, that's the situation.

Now the voices of people inside the church are much louder than those outside the church. Because of its prominent location, the people of the community pass by the church's campus on a daily basis, but the ministry is completely disconnected from the community.

The senior pastor was hired because of his strong pastoral gifts rather than his ability to champion a new vision for the future. The church wanted a caretaker rather than a leader.

The ministry leaders, including both the staff and volunteers, are solely focused on their specific ministry areas. They've learned to guard their turf. There's no unified mission, vision, and strategy for the church to return to health.

Everything is pulling to that past. The people who have been around the church for decades remember when the church was vibrant, and they want to take the church back to that time even though the community and the culture continue to move in a new direction.

This is a challenging season for churches because the signs of decline and lack of health become obvious, but the pain typically isn't bad enough to foster a desire for change. I wish I could offer more hope here, but many churches in this phase of the life cycle will eventually continue down toward life support and eventually death.

But that doesn't always have to be the case. Sometimes the church can begin a transition that returns the ministry to health and growth. I will try to unpack some of the key strategies required for churches to begin that journey. The key, though, is that change will be required. You can't preserve the past and expect to go to a new place of health in the future.

If your church is at this place, I hope you are praying for your church. I hope you are praying for your leaders. I hope you are praying for your community. Prayer is foundational in every season of the church's journey but maybe more so in this season.

Why do I say that? Because it's really not possible for us to change someone else's heart. Only God can produce heart change.

That's what, ultimately, is required for churches in preservation. The church's heart must change. The people in the church must change. There must be a revival within the church for it to return to health and growth. Only this isn't a scheduled revival with a guest speaker scheduled for the third week of July. It's not an event. Rather it's a spiritual transformation that the people of a church experience, and it shifts their focus from playing church to reaching people for Jesus.

For the church to return to sustained health, a growing core of people needs to come to the realization that church isn't about *me*. My preferences aren't as important as the people we are trying to reach. My needs aren't as important as those outside the church. My faith is meaningless if it isn't backed by actions to carry out God's mission.

As a growing core of people come to that realization, it's possible that God can begin to do a new work in a church. That's a change, though, that can't be forced on people. God needs to move in people's hearts. Gifted leaders can help prepare people for this journey, but prayer for heart change and a spiritual reawakening will be essential. The hope and prayer should be that enough people grow discontent with playing church that you start to see an urgency for change to develop.

But if you think you need to wait for everyone to get to that place, you'll never change. At some point you'll have to determine when you have enough key people ready to move forward with the necessary changes to return the church to health and growth. Leaders, again, will see this first. They'll know before anyone else in the congregation can see it. You can't forget, though, that faith demands action.

Let me tell you the story of Piedmont Church near Atlanta,

Georgia. When Dr. Ike Reighard became the senior pastor in 2006, he faced a challenging situation. For the previous decade, the church had been in decline. The congregation was still holding on to a ministry strategy that had worked well in the past, when the church was thriving. At the point when Ike took over, though, the ministry was clearly in preservation mode.

"My first step was to create a sense of urgency based on data which helped to take the emotions out of decisions that needed to be made," said Ike. We'll talk more about how leaders begin by using urgency to lead change later, but this was a critical step. Rather than blaming the previous leaders, Ike used the data he collected from the prior decade to define the current reality. That provided the foundation for what would come next.

The next step was to cast a vision for a better future. Ike launched the new vision through a teaching series. He explained, "I called the series 'Courageous Conversations,' and I based the messages out of the book of Nehemiah. Having a strong biblical context is essential when you desire change in a church setting." While this was happening, Ike was also working with the elders, some of the key influencers of the church, to unify around the vision.

Then they started to implement some key changes. One of the most significant was reengaging their community. Over the years, the church had become very inward-focused. They began looking for every opportunity they could to serve in the community. "Piedmont Church had become virtually invisible and had lost its impact in the community," explained Ike. "Sometimes we became fixated on being the best church in our community, rather than being the best church *for* our community."

While they were reconnecting with the community, the

church also had some internal challenges to address, primarily their facilities. Like the church itself, the facilities had been in decline for years. There were many maintenance issues, and the interior decor was dated by several decades. The church had to invest a significant amount of money to repair and renovate their facilities.

As they were implementing these changes, Ike looked for opportunities to celebrate the wins along the way. He shared, "When people celebrate together, it creates a sense of energy, excitement, and engagement. No matter how small the victory, taking time to recognize it is essential."

Ike admitted, though, it hasn't all been easy. Any change comes with challenges. For churches, regardless of how good and healthy the change is, it means that some people will leave during the process. Ike explained the ups and downs of the journey this way: "When we started implementing the changes at Piedmont, I knew that we would dip down further in attendance before we would ever start moving upward. Change is difficult for people, and we made radical changes that caused a significant loss of members. One of these changes was eliminating a choir, which deeply offended some of the membership. Other changes were also viewed as negative by some inside the church, but others outside the church were now being attracted to the new Piedmont."[1]

Piedmont Church has become a new ministry over the last decade. They went from being a church in decline for many years to a church that's experiencing vibrancy and growth once again. They went from a church entrenched in the preservation mode to a ministry that's experiencing new life. It can happen in your church as well.

With that, let me share some of the characteristics of churches that are stuck in the preservation phase. In each of these instances, we need to identify patterns that are established over a long period of time—years not months.

1. *Attendance and finances are both declining.* In the maintenance phase, attendance may plateau or begin to decline. Now attendance drop will become noticeable. Not only are new guests not keeping pace with the natural turnover due to moves, deaths, and other life transitions, but people are starting to leave specifically to attend other churches. As people leave, so does their giving. The church may have trouble staying current on bills and may have to reduce staff to deal with the financial decline.

2. *Methods become more important than the mission.* This is when the real worship wars occur as people prioritize their own stylistic preferences above those the church is trying to reach. People dig in their heels regarding service times, Sunday school classes, programs, and events that have been around for years. Turf wars become the norm as ministries stake their claims on budget, space, staff, volunteers, and other resources. The ministry silos become entrenched.

3. *There's a prevailing pull to go back to the way things used to be.* This pull gets stronger as newer people leave for other churches and the number of people connected to the church declines. The people who have been around the longest also have more staying power, and their voices become louder. Remembering how healthy the

church was in the past, generations of people who may have once been open to change now call for returning to the methods that worked before.

4. *The strong leaders and visionaries have left the church.* I say this in the past tense because they probably actually have been gone for some time. It doesn't take long for good leaders to realize that the church is not moving forward. When that occurs, leaders, particularly leaders with a big vision for what the church could be, get antsy and start looking for other opportunities. The challenge, of course, is that these are the same people who would most benefit a church in the preservation season.

5. *Power shifts from the pastor and staff to the lay leadership.* By this point, it's not uncommon for a church to have experienced transitions in pastoral and staff leadership. During those transition seasons, the remaining lay leaders will often try to take control. Again, this is a natural preservation tactic. They'll shift power and decision making from the staff to boards and committees. This often also shapes their hiring decisions when they go to fill pastoral and staff positions. They'll try to find leaders who are willing to serve more in a pastoral capacity rather than using leadership gifts.

6. *The focus shifts to keeping people from leaving.* Whereas the churches on the upside of the life cycle are focused on reaching new people, the churches in preservation mode are just trying to keep the people they have. That's a defensive posture, and it won't help the church return to sustained health.

Here's the good news. It's possible to transition churches out of this preservation phase. It doesn't happen often, but it can work. I'm going to move forward with the assumption that you've heeded my advice and started to pray for your church and its leaders. I'm going to assume you have a developing urgency in your people to chart a new course. If that's the case, then let's unpack some of the next steps that will be required for you to return to church health.

Change Demands Intentional Leadership: You Can't Keep Everyone Happy and Experience the Change That Produces Health

Tradition is powerful. When a church has experienced success, the motivation for change can be low or even nonexistent. The assumption here is that a church has, at some point in the past, experienced sustained health, but now they're on the downside of the life cycle. By the time they hit this preservation phase, tradition becomes even more powerful.

Change can be time consuming, frustrating, and even costly. It is much easier to avoid change as long as possible. Eventually some churches are willing to change when the pain associated with status quo becomes greater than the pain associated with change. Pain is the key. Frankly, even for churches, pain often isn't felt until there's a financial crisis. This is when the change cycle begins.

I think most leaders are guilty of thinking if they lead really, really well, then everyone will stick with them. Reality says you'll lose people after each phase of implementing change. Let me prepare you for the journey ahead by walking you through the cycles of change you will experience.

Cycle One: Creating Urgency

The change cycle begins when the leader demonstrates the need for change. You create urgency by explaining why the change is necessary to execute and why it can't wait.

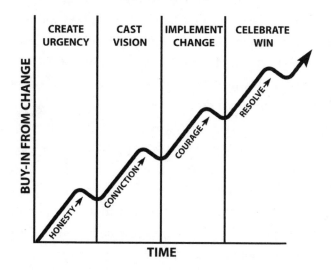

During this cycle, some people, out of pride, will certainly oppose change. Possibly the change affects an area they have previously led or are currently carrying. Other people experience fear. They worry they may lose their significance or they possibly feel anxious over the financial risks of the change.

In this part of the change cycle, leaders have to be ruthlessly honest. You need to help people understand that the pain of staying where you are is much more harmful than the pain you'll experience by going through the change. People need to hear the truth. They may not embrace the truth, but the leader needs to provide it.

The challenge, of course, is that leaders often see the truth before anyone else does. It's part of the unique wiring God puts in you as a leader. It's one of the key reasons why you are the leader and others are not. Leaders see it first.

Cycle Two: Cast a Vision

This is the time for the change to be communicated to all levels of the organization. You have to connect whatever changes you are making to the mission and vision of the church. Once the leadership team believes the change has been communicated, it should be communicated again and again. The person at the lowest level of leadership should have an understanding of the change that is taking place.

During this cycle, tension can sometimes be felt among leaders, volunteers, and church members. This is a time when disgruntled people begin forming alliances to make a final push to stop the change from happening. Depending on the size of the change, some people will stop giving or even threaten to leave. I've noticed it's very easy for church leaders to overestimate the level of negativity toward the change. Fear is often louder than reality.

At this point in the change process, leaders need to paint the picture of where you are going in the future. You need to cast a vision, and it must be clear and compelling. Any strong vision begins with the conviction deep in a leader's heart. *You* must believe in the change before anyone else will believe in the change.

Many times change fails, though, because leaders neglect this step. They jump immediately to implementation without expressing the *why* that is driving the decision. You need to rally people around the vision first.

Cycle Three: Implement the Change

There will always be people who want to wait to see how things are going. They're neither committed nor ready to leave, but after you've actually made the change, these people will test the waters to determine whether or not the leaders will actually follow through. Not unlike raising children, you have to establish boundaries and stick to them. If someone starts to create division because they don't like the change, you have to address it immediately. The hope is that they'll embrace unity with the rest of the team. But if their desire is to create division and harm, then they may have to be encouraged to leave.

This is when leaders become leaders. Until this point, change has only been a conversation. Now it's time for implementation. In these moments, fear can become very loud. Who will disagree? Who will get angry? Who will leave? This is when courage is required.

There are days when I hate the fact that God created me with a strategic mind. When I'm the one in control of those gifts, I can easily fall into a trap where I jump to the worst possible scenarios. When God is the one in control, though, I'm able to see the potential. Ironically, when I have the courage to take the leap, my worst fears are never realized.

This is another example of how pride is the enemy of courage. When fear or worry creeps into my thoughts, I'm admitting that I believe I am in control. Courage begins when I humbly acknowledge that "he must become greater and greater, and I must become less and less" (John 3:30).

Cycle Four: Celebrate Early Wins

Wise leaders are quick to celebrate wins that happen from the change. Many people will jump on board when they see the change is working in a timely, visible, and meaningful way. Slow change is rarely positive change, so sharing quick wins will build morale and take away power from critics.

When I was a kid, I remember climbing into the "way back" of the family station wagon for long car trips. On those trips I generally knew the destination Dad had in mind, but I also lacked the patience to quietly enjoy the journey. It wouldn't be very long into the trip before I'd ask for the first of many, many times, "Are we there yet?"

Now that I have four kids of my own, I know that question is deeply rooted in the human psyche. When we set out on a journey to a new destination, there's something in each one of us that wants to know whether or not we're making progress. That's why it's so important to celebrate the early wins.

The challenge for leaders, though, is that they're rarely satisfied until the final destination is reached. That's why leaders need resolve. Without resolve, the leader will tend to jump from challenge to challenge, from new idea to new idea, without seeing a change fully through to completion.

Additionally, resolve is needed for all the dips along the way. Though healthy change ultimately leads to a healthier destination, it's not uncommon to lose people along the way. In fact, it's in this final stage of the change cycle you are most likely to lose the people who have been with you the longest. They believed in you for a time, but the change hasn't yet generated the results they expect and their patience has worn out. That's when you'll really need the resolve to see the change through to completion.

Let me say it again: when a major change is being executed, some people will inevitably leave. It's a natural part of change. If the church has made it this far down the life cycle toward life support, then major change will be required. In other words, you can't try to keep everyone happy *and* make the changes required to return to sustained health. People will leave the church. If your goal is to keep everyone happy and connected to the church, then you might as well skip to the next chapter about churches on life support, because that's where you will end up.

Wrong expectations sabotage your perception of success when leading change—and your expectations set those of the people you lead. When leaders worry about the people who leave, they are not focusing on the new people who will eventually come as a result of the change. Remember, you are stewarding a God-given mission. If you try to make everyone happy, the mission isn't the priority.

You can't afford to waste time and energy on those who have no longer bought into the vision. This is actually a time to celebrate. Some endings have to happen in order to open the door to a brighter and better future.

Address the Warning Signs First: You Can't Ignore Problems and Expect Them to Go Away

By now, I'm actually hopeful that churches recognize that they're legitimately stuck. If so, there's hope. When churches feel stuck, they're ready for change.

When I started what eventually became The Unstuck Group back in 2009, I had lots of people providing great advice about how I should approach helping churches. I distinctly remember a couple of people telling me to define clearly what I was going to offer churches and then focus on that. So I did. I knew my thing was strategy. I knew that was a personal strength of my leadership. I had been writing about it for years. I decided I was going to provide strategy to churches.

Well, that worked to some extent, but only enough to keep me busy. That wasn't my vision. My vision included building a team of people with lots of years of ministry experience to serve hundreds of churches in any given year. I was only helping six or seven churches at a time by trying to offer strategy. My vision had stalled.

That's when I realized I had to take a spoonful of my own medicine. For years I had been challenging churches and teaching pastors to address the felt needs of their audiences. I expressed how it's hard to teach biblical truth until you've given someone a reason to listen. You need to stick to biblical truth, but you need to hook the felt needs of the person you are trying to reach.

I wasn't doing that. I was trying to force strategic planning on churches without acknowledging the felt needs of the church leaders who were needing my help. I realized they weren't looking for strategy, even though I knew they needed it. They were feeling stuck. That was the word that continually popped up in just about every conversation I was having with pastors and other church leaders. "We're stuck."

So I started to ask more questions. "Why do you feel that way?" As I engaged with churches through our ministry health assessment process, I began to document the common barriers. "What led to the decline you are experiencing?" I talked with others who engaged with churches that were plateaued and declining, particularly leaders within mainline denominations. "What are the common issues you see in churches that are struggling?"

I confirmed the felt need. Church leaders were feeling stuck. That's when I began to shift the language I was using and the approach I was taking. Instead of trying to sell strategy, the focus became helping churches get unstuck. That's when The Unstuck Group really took off.

Out of that process, I discovered five key characteristics of churches that were stuck. Churches can, of course, get stuck at any point along the life cycle. I'm not talking about that kind of stuck here. Instead, I'm talking about really being *stuck*. The church is declining in attendance. The baptisms are slowing or nonexistent. The spiritual climate within the church is dead. If the trend continues, the church will eventually have to close its doors. I'm talking about that kind of stuck.

In those instances, there are five common factors that contribute to the decline.

1. *They Lack a Focused, Compelling Vision for the Future*
   The church needs a vision for the future in order to remain healthy. It needs to be specific. It needs to be big enough to rally people to the cause. I've shared with churches that the vision needs to be big enough that it can't be accomplished in your own effort, but realistic enough that it could happen through a move of God. The vision, though, is what keeps everyone pointed in the same direction. Churches that lack vision tend to drift back to doing what they've always done. You can't do what you've always done and expect different results.

2. *They Don't Have a Clear Discipleship Path*
   Rather than a path, churches have a collection of ministry programs. All those programs are usually targeted to various subgroups. There are separate activities for kids, students, and adults of different ages. There are separate activities for singles, married couples without kids, married couples with kids, divorcees, and empty nesters. The calendar of activities keeps people busy, but it reinforces the consumer mind-set that you'd expect to fade as people take up their cross to follow Christ.

Instead, churches need to develop a path that everyone takes to move from where they are to where God wants them to be.

3. *They Have an Inward Focus*

Almost everything the church does is for people who are already connected to the church. Worship services are for church people. Classes are for church people. Small groups are for church people. Events are for church people. It's impossible for any church to be healthy and experience growth if nothing they do is designed to reach people who are outside the faith and outside the church. There needs to be a healthy balance of ministry initiatives and environments designed to reach people outside the faith and encourage next steps for those who have committed their lives to following Jesus. In other words, the church needs to establish an intentional strategy to shift to an outward focus.

4. *They Are Complex*

Complexity comes in several shapes and sizes. Some churches are complex because of the amount of programming they have in place. Some are complex because of the competing messages they are trying to communicate. Others are complex because of the structure and systems they've established. With numerous boards and committees in place, decision making gets complicated and slows down to the point that it becomes almost impossible for the church to move forward. Healthy churches reduce the programming clutter, focus communications, and streamline structure and decision-making. This allows more ministry to happen and more lives to be positively impacted.

5. *They Don't Have Strong Leadership*

I see two flavors of this issue. The first is a situation where people, including senior pastors, who don't have the leadership gift are in leadership positions. Whenever any part of the body of Christ is performing a role they were not designed to engage, it's going to create a problem. The body will not be healthy. Leadership positions demand leadership gifts.

The second situation I see is when people with leadership gifts aren't empowered to use them, because the structure and systems constrain them. For example, I've run into instances when a church board sees it as their responsibility to keep the senior pastor in line. That's not the role of the board. Among other things, the board should be equipping and empowering the pastor to use his leadership gifts. God designed leaders to lead.

I drive an eleven-year-old vehicle. I do that on purpose, because there are other places I'd rather be investing money than in an automobile that simply gets me from here to there. The challenge with driving an older car, though, is that it tends to need more maintenance. Though that's still cheaper than a car payment, I can't just ignore the warning lights that show up on my dashboard. If I were to continually disregard those warnings, the car would eventually stop working. I would have to start all over by purchasing another vehicle.

I tried that with a different car once. I had an old Audi A6. I loved that car, but after several years the warning lights seemed to pop up daily. Instead of taking the car to a garage and letting a mechanic fix the issues, I cut a piece of black electrical tape and covered up the warnings. Out of sight, out of mind. Guess what. That strategy didn't work. The problems didn't fix themselves. After several months, I ended up with a vehicle that needed thousands of dollars' worth of repairs—far more than the car was worth. My car had to go to Audi heaven.

The same holds true for the five factors mentioned above. You can consider each of them as warning lights for churches. If one turns on, that should get your attention. If more than one is flashing, you have a problem. If all of them are lit up, it's a crisis.

Here's the challenge: most churches who find themselves in this stage of the life cycle are focusing on preserving what they've always done in the past. That's how this stage gets its name. When the warning lights start to turn on, I see churches trying to cover up the warnings rather than dealing with the problems. They're hoping they'll just go away.

That's when leaders need to step up and take the first steps in leading the change I mentioned earlier. Someone has to be honest and state the truth. If the warning lights are on, the ministry is not healthy. It's time to identify a new direction and embrace changes that will breathe new life into the church.

Look Backward to Move Forward: The Key to Health May Be in the Rearview Mirror

Since I'm a guy with futuristic and strategic strengths, you might be surprised to hear this advice from me. What I've learned, though, is that it always helps to look back if you want to move forward. What I mean by looking backward is looking to your past.

Whenever I begin a strategic planning process with a church, I always start by helping the leadership team look to the past. We unpack the history of the church. What was the original vision that shaped the early years? What values did the leadership embrace in the past? How has the leadership and culture shifted through the years? What ministries of the church had the biggest impact? How have the congregation and the community changed through the years? There's a lot that can be learned from the church's past. History is important.

As we map out what happened in the past, we try to identify the key moments that shifted the direction of the ministry. We look for trends and common themes. We look for how these critical points impacted the church's health.

I've found that this process of looking back is particularly important for churches in this preservation season. When we dig into the history, it helps bring clarity and focus for the future. For starters, it gives us an opportunity to honor the people who shaped the history of the church. That's essential. If they weren't there, their friends and family may have been part of some of those critical moments. It's healthy to pause and recognize how God used these people to have an important impact on the church's ministry. Healthy honor helps to build trust. You need trust to implement change.

Second, it helps us to discover when the church was healthiest and what contributed to that health. It's not uncommon to hear things like this as we review the history together:

"There was more unity when we had a clear, compelling vision."

"Our church used to be more focused on reaching new people. We've lost our evangelistic priority."

"When our leadership was healthy, the church was healthy and it experienced growth."

"We had more success engaging volunteers when we had fewer competing programs."

Great athletes do this. When they find themselves in a slump, they'll get with their coach and review film together. They'll watch video from the past, when performance was up. They're looking for what has changed in their performance that may be contributing to the current slump. The best golfers routinely do this with their swing. They'll slow the video down to one frame at a time to review the position of their body, their hands, and the club and compare this with past videos.

This is what we do with churches too. We slow down the video of the church's history to figure out what has changed along the way. We look at what has shifted that may be contributing to where the church is in its life cycle. That helps us to uncover the core issues that need to be addressed so the church can return to health.

Looking to the past also helps uncover the values that shaped previous ministry strategy. That's important, because a church's values should rarely change. Unfortunately, there are times when the church drifts away from the core values that once produced fruit. Instead of holding on to this foundational focus, the methods for doing ministry become more important. One way to introduce change is to return to the mission and values that once produced health.

One example of this occurred with a church I worked with several years ago. We were in the process of reviewing the church's history when one of the older gentlemen spoke up. He had been at the church for many decades. He's the guy you really want in the room when you are trying to glean the critical truths about the church's past.

There were about fifteen people seated around a conference table, representing both the staff and lay leaders. This gentleman talked about a time several decades ago when the church used to be healthy and growing. During that season, one of the most effective strategies they used was door-to-door evangelism. A group of people would gather at the church on a Tuesday evening. They'd eat together, pray, and then canvas the neighborhoods. They would knock on doors, initiate conversations, and share with people about Jesus. They would conclude each conversation with an invitation to join the church.

This used to be an effective evangelism strategy in many churches. It's possible it may still work for you too. But it's been many years since I've found a church that was using door-to-door evangelism to effectively reach new people for Jesus. Our society is very different today. Door-to-door sales used to be a common strategy for many businesses. Today, physical stores and the Internet have replaced that approach. Today, we live in gated communities. We don't answer the front door unless we're expecting guests. We don't answer the phone unless we know who is calling. Rather than rushing to answer the knock, we see it as an intrusion.

The older man who had been at the church for many, many years was advocating they return to door-to-door evangelism. He remembered the church as healthy when they used that strategy, so he wanted to start that ministry again. Eventually the team realized they couldn't return to that method because the culture had changed, but they needed to return to the values that drove that strategy.

The underlying value was a heart for evangelism. They wanted to reach people outside the faith and outside the church. They wanted people to experience the hope, forgiveness, and love found only in Jesus Christ. They wanted more people to be a part of their church too. We used this exercise of unpacking this history to reignite a value that used to be a priority but, in the decades since, had waned.

Your gut may tell you that looking back is not a wise approach to moving forward. If all you do is look back, then that would be true. By looking to the past, though, we can appropriately celebrate and honor what God has previously blessed. We can learn from what worked and identify issues that have developed. We can return to the mission and values that once produced fruit. The practice of looking back isn't to return to what the church used to do; it's to return to what God wants the church to be.

Structure Boards for Health and Impact: Move More People into Ministry over Meetings

As churches are moving up the life cycle toward sustained health, I've noticed that most of their structure challenges typically revolve around staffing decisions. With churches moving down the life cycle and away from sustained health, the more common structure challenge seems to be with governance, including boards and committees. Healthy, growing churches tend to have fewer boards and committees. Declining churches tend to have many boards and committees.

One example of this was a church I worked with that had been declining for a number of years. They had about seven hundred people attending the church, but the governing board had fifty people on it. They also had twelve different committees. It was so complicated, they had to have a committee to determine who was on committees. I can't remember the last time I found a church on the upside of the life cycle with that much complexity. Unfortunately, it's common among churches in decline.

It's probably no surprise to you that the common challenge of churches with a complex governance structure is that they lack unity and trust. We could probably argue whether the structure is the cause or the effect. Either way, there appears to be a correlation and an opportunity for churches to return to health by finding a better way to structure the leadership and decision making.

A church was struggling in this area during a preservation season. The church was in an older building that needed some facility updates. They couldn't afford a major renovation, but they had plenty of resources to make some cosmetic changes. One change the staff leadership identified was that the space used on a weekly basis by the student ministry needed a fresh coat of paint. But before they could paint the room, they had to get approval from the youth ministry committee, the trustees, the finance committee, and the board. Every time they put something to a vote, though, there were questions along the way. And here's why: people in power need to justify their existence.

I don't recall which one, but the decision to paint the student space became stuck in one committee even though the other committees approved. Eventually someone got fed up, purchased some paint, and painted the room on their own. This is not the way leadership and decision making should look.

With that, here are some of the best practices I've noticed in churches that are moving toward sustained health. It begins with having only one lay leadership board, which should be made up of five to nine people, depending on the size of the church. Eliminate all other boards and committees. This board sticks to the big picture, and it doesn't get involved in the day-to-day ministry decisions, which are the pastor's and the staff's responsibility.

The board's primary responsibilities include modeling spiritual leadership for the rest of the congregation and providing encouragement to the senior pastor. In that role, it should be more about empowerment than accountability; however, the board and the pastor should work together to establish healthy boundaries for the pastor's soul, marriage, family, and leadership.

The board should also be engaged in big-picture decisions that shape the church's mission, vision, and values. When it comes to defining ministry strategy, though, that responsibility belongs to the pastor and staff. If there's a healthy relationship established with trust and unity, it won't be unusual for the pastor to seek guidance and wisdom from the board on big strategic shifts.

The board should focus on decisions that are significant in scope, like approving the annual budget, setting the pastor's salary, purchasing land, or building new facilities. The pastor and staff should be responsible for day-to-day operations, including any purchases approved by the board in the annual budget. The board should monitor finances, but it's the professional staff's responsibility to manage the finances.

The board should oversee only one person—the senior pastor. That means the senior pastor has the responsibility of hiring, managing, coaching, directing, and, if needed, firing anyone in a staff role. If a senior pastor demonstrates an inability to handle these responsibilities, the board's recourse is to find another pastor. It is a far better separation of roles, though, to clearly define the leadership structure and decision-making authority. It's hard for a pastor to effectively lead a staff who are hired and fired by someone else.

I highly recommend you eliminate congregational voting for members of this board. There is no biblical foundation for voting on church leaders. Instead, I'd encourage you to use a system where the pastor and the senior staff recommend board candidates and the existing board affirms new board members. This prevents a situation where people are voting on the most popular people in the congregation to serve in spiritual leadership positions. Sometimes the most popular person isn't the most spiritually ready for leadership. They may have sin issues in their lives that would prevent them from being biblically qualified to lead. They may not even be Christ followers. Besides that, voting has a tendency to divide people rather than unite them.

Shifting to a solution where board members are selected without a church vote also helps to eliminate the sense that everyone should have a voice in every decision. We want biblically qualified, spiritually mature believers making decisions. The church was never designed to be a democracy.

More important than anything else I've mentioned, though, is the fact that simplifying governance helps move more people into ministry and out of meetings. I'm tired of seeing occasions where people gather once a month to decide what the ministry staff should or shouldn't do. If you can't trust your pastor and your staff to make wise decisions in line with the church's mission, vision, and values, then you need to find another pastor. I'd much rather have people invest their time, gifts, and energy in making disciples than in making decisions in a church committee meeting.

Prioritize the Main Thing: Adding More Events to the Calendar Will Not Produce Church Health

One of the common tactics I see in churches once they get to this place in the life cycle is to try to "event" their way back to health and growth. I think one of the primary reasons why that happens is because churches are grasping at straws by this point. They're trying to find that magic bullet to turn things around. Rather than making the necessary changes to leadership and strategy that may cause some people to be unhappy, it's just easier to add an event to the calendar. Here are a few more reasons why churches add more and more events to the calendar:

- Churches do events because churches have always done events. It doesn't matter if the event actually helps people or not, they do the event because they're supposed to do the event.
- Churches do events because they're easy to measure. If more people show up, they assume the event was successful and helpful.
- Churches do events because leaders are lazy. It's a lot easier to throw events on the calendar than it is to think about how they might effectively help people take their next steps, especially if that involves engaging people in relationships.
- Churches do events because they justify staff positions. Staff members feel obligated to do events to prove the need for their positions.
- Churches do events because leaders have egos. It feels

good to get up in front of a group of people and teach them. They feel more fulfilled.

- Churches do events because they're afraid to say no. Many times they don't know *when* to say no, because they haven't established a clear vision and strategy.

Whatever the case, churches tend to become very event-driven over time. Every time the church wants people to take a next step, they schedule an event. Then, when people don't show up at their events, they assume people are either unspiritual or uncommitted.

The reality is that your supposedly successful event could actually be doing quite a bit of harm. If you keep people busy at your events, you may be preventing them from investing in their marriage, their children, and their relationships with other people, including people outside the faith. You may be preventing them from fulfilling their calling. They think they're becoming more Christlike by going to church, but you could actually be pulling them away from what God has called them to do.

Several years ago I created the following chart to help determine whether or not an event was healthy. In fact, I've heard church leaders mention that they've saved this and used it to make sure they're doing events on purpose and for a purpose. This might be a tool you use, as events are being scheduled, to filter out any events that won't produce health. And you can use this as a tool after the event to debrief your team.

If you haven't done so in the past, then now would be a good time to list every event your church offers in the calendar year. Then, as a team, assess whether or not it's healthy. Use this as an opportunity either to get the unhealthy events in the healthy column or, if that's not possible, consider stopping the unhealthy events. Whatever you do, don't continue scheduling the event because you've always done it. That's one of the reasons why events are killing the church.

Healthy Events	Unhealthy Events
The win is helping people take a next step after the event.	The win is getting people to show up to the event.
The target audience is people who haven't connected to the church or ministry.	The target audience is people who have already connected to the church or ministry.
The primary way people hear about the event is through the invitation of a friend.	The primary way people hear about the event is through promotions.
Volunteer teams own the event.	Staff teams own the event.
Events are prioritized so people are encouraged to stay connected in their other community engagements.	Events are scheduled to force people to choose church over other community engagements.
Since guests are expected, every element of the experience is planned with that in mind.	Since guests are not expected, certain elements don't need as much attention.
You capture pictures and video to share the stories of people who were impacted by the event.	You capture pictures and video to share the story of the event itself.
After the event, there's a debrief to make sure the win was accomplished.	After the event, you communicate how many people showed up.
Every year the events are evaluated to make sure they are still fulfilling their primary purpose.	Every year the events are scheduled because they're expected.
The event is scheduled again to connect new people to the church.	The event is scheduled again to keep people from leaving the church.

Then, moving forward, the next time you are tempted to launch a new event, first ask, If we were forced to do something other than an event, how might we help people take their next steps toward Christ? By forcing that constraint, you might discover other options that could produce more fruit and require much smaller investments of time and resources than putting one more thing on the calendar.

That said, there may be times when an event is the right call. My caution is that you not overplay that tactic. Here's my guess: if you get aggressive about eliminating events on your church calendars, the alternatives for helping people take their next steps are going to look a lot like the discipleship relationships we see modeled in the Bible. The more you can help people move into relationships centered in Christ, the stronger and healthier your church is going to be.

If your church is in the preservation phase of the life cycle, it's going to require some critical shifts to help the ministry return to health and growth. Specifically, I mentioned the importance of leading strong, addressing the key warning signs, rediscovering what made the church healthy in the past, restructuring the governing board, and prioritizing the events on the church's calendar. None of this is easy, but all of it is necessary in order to avoid declining further to life support. That's the last phase of the life cycle I will unpack in the final chapter.

CHAPTER 7

LIFE SUPPORT

It's Time to Embrace a New Beginning

In some respects, this is the portion of the book I was least looking forward to writing. This chapter is focused on churches that have entered the life support season of the life cycle. In other words, they're near death. The doors of the church are about ready to close. If a church doesn't address the core issues preventing health in the maintenance and preservation seasons, they're guaranteed to end up here.

No one likes to talk about death, but for some churches it will be the natural next step. In fact, I think it's more than likely that a church will end up closing its doors if they've survived until the life support phase. That's not always the case, though, and that's why there's a part of me that's hopeful when I find a church that recognizes they are on life support.

There are other factors that lead to churches getting to this place, but primary among them is this challenge: the church wants to reach new people and remain financially viable while holding on to their old methods. In the previous stages of the life cycle, this condition began to creep into the culture. Now this attribute becomes pervasive. It drives everything. And if left unchecked, it will ultimately lead to the church's demise.

If a church, however, acknowledges that the end is near, then sometimes they're willing to do something dramatic to turn things around. It will indeed take something dramatic. The reality is that churches on life support need to somehow find their way back to a new beginning. They need to start over. We'll talk later about the different ways this might happen, but the church can't survive at this point without a relaunch.

Here's the story of a church that overcame the odds and found a new beginning. Solid Ground Church in Lewes, Delaware, is on the Delaware Bay. This area has been challenging for ministries throughout the years. In fact, the Association of Religion Data Archives has reported that less than 10 percent of Sussex County, where Lewes is situated, is part of an evangelical church. The majority of the remaining 90 percent are not connected to any church at all.[1]

Pastor Burt Miller has lived in Lewes most of his life. He planted the church in 2009. For the first six years, the church couldn't get more than eighty people to attend. They were stuck.

That's when our team was introduced to Burt. You need to know, though, that this isn't a story about The Unstuck Group. Instead, this is a story about a leader and a church who were willing to make significant changes in order to experience a new beginning. Our team can give counsel and coaching, but the church leaders on the ground need to have the courage to lead through the change.

Burt helped the church clarify its mission and vision. This helped the church better understand its identity and uniqueness. He also helped the church understand why they do what they do. That's an important first step. If you jump to changes in methodology before you answer why you do what you do, then the changes, no matter how healthy they might be, are rarely going to take hold.

After confirming their vision and their identity, the most significant change the church made was to relocate. For anyone who has led a church through a relocation effort in the past, you know the challenge this presents. Burt helped the congregation see that they needed to move in order to meet their community where they live. Who they were trying to reach became more important than who they were trying to keep.

As you might guess, though, not everyone bought into the vision and the changes that went with it. Some people left the church because they couldn't get on board with the vision. Others left the church because of the relocation. In other words, the church took a few steps backward before they could move forward.

The loss of people is the primary reason churches would rather die than change. They know that if they change, they will likely lose some people who are already connected to the church. If you make changes that really matter, then you will certainly lose people. The opposite, however, is true as well. If you never change, you will also eventually lose people. The challenge is that the voices in the first instance are always louder. People who leave because the church doesn't change usually go quietly. The difference, of course, is that healthy change also has the potential to generate new growth. It will likely take some pruning in order for the church to begin to bear new fruit.

Thankfully, Burt was a strong leader through this season, and now the church is experiencing new life. The church is the healthiest it's ever been. They're seeing people accept Christ and get baptized. Small groups are multiplying. New leaders are being raised up. Giving has increased dramatically. People who haven't been to church in years are connecting and getting plugged into serving roles. The church has recently added a second worship service, and they've grown to 170 people in attendance. Solid Ground has started a brand-new life cycle. They've launched all over again.

With the inspiration from a church that made the necessary changes to move from life support to a new beginning, let me point out some of the key characteristics of churches that find themselves in this place on the life cycle:

1. *They are unwilling to change.* As I mentioned previously, this is the primary factor that leads to a church's entering the life support phase. The priority focus is around maintaining everything the way it's always been rather than reaching new people. If the church can't get past this barrier, it will eventually die.

2. *There is no fruit.* New people rarely, if ever, connect to the church. It's not uncommon for the church to go years without any adults accepting Christ and being baptized. If there is spiritual formation happening in individuals, it isn't translating in any engagement of the Great Commission.

3. *The church is being led by one key family or one key donor.* Anyone else with any leadership capacity has typically left for another ministry by this point. The future really hinges on what these key influencers do next. If they eventually get to the place where they're willing to acknowledge it's not about them, then there's a chance the church will survive. If not, these same leaders will be the people who eventually turn out the lights for the last time.

4. *They are typically experiencing financial crisis.* I wish the lack of fruit in evangelism and discipleship was the

primary cause for crisis. Unfortunately, I've seen way too many churches willing to overlook that as long as they could pay the bills and keep the building open. By the time the church arrives at life support, though, the financial crisis begins to take hold. That can be a good thing, though, if it finally prompts the church to act and embrace the significant changes that are required.

5. *The church is aging.* Though not always the case, churches in life support are typically older. The church itself is older and so are the people who remain in the church. This stands to reason because the older generation is holding on to the traditions that are preventing it from becoming a new church with new life. Every generation will face this challenge. Each has to decide whether or not they'll sacrifice personal preferences in order to reach the next generations.

6. *The blame game takes root.* Rather than face reality and make ministry changes that could propel the church back to health, the remaining leaders begin to blame others. It might be people within the church who want to embrace a new vision or ministry strategy. They may blame the culture for shifting away from God. They may blame other churches for stealing people away from their church. Once this spirit takes root, it's difficult to eliminate.

Though it's my prayer you will never be in a church that is on life support, I do want to equip you with a few tools and provide some hope. The church on life support can experience new life and a new beginning. I've seen it happen, but I need to be honest with you: it's going to take a significant shift in ministry philosophy and strategy, and without a doubt, it's going to take a move of God. With that, let me unpack some potential next steps to return to ministry health.

Embrace a New Mission: Begin by Reestablishing Why the Church Exists

Back when my family and I were much younger, we were out of town on a Sunday and not able to attend our church. While we were gone, we went to a service at a church that was much different from the one we belonged to back home. There were only three Morgan kids at the time, and they were all under the age of ten. Because this church didn't have children's ministry available, they joined us in the sanctuary.

That should tell you a lot about who I am. I'm always looking to experience new things. I don't like physical risks, but I do take risks. That includes going to churches that might be different from my normal. I'm always hopeful I'll learn something new or, at the very least, confirm that I'm part of a great church.

Because of the focus on children's ministry at our home church, our kids had grown accustomed to ministry environments with lots of energy, current music, video, relevant teaching, and lots and lots of new people. Because this church experience was going to be very different, I was interested to see how they would respond.

The church we were visiting had been around for more than a century. Learning a little bit about the history of the congregation, we found that at one time the church had been very vibrant, with many young families. That wasn't the case, though, at the time we visited. There were very few people our age. The facility was dated. They used very traditional music. The message was boring for both my kids and for me.

My son, Jacob, was only six at the time. He's always been perceptive and expressive. It was no surprise then that he had something to share after the service was over. As we were walking out of the church, Jacob tugged on my sleeve and quietly said what everyone else in the family was thinking. "Dad, this church is never going to grow."

He was right. The church was dying. It was on life support. I'm sure there were a number of contributing factors that ultimately led to the decline, but I'm convinced that among the most critical was the fact that the church lost focus on its mission.

Remember the conversation about mission? I talked about this at the very beginning of the journey through the life cycle of a church. For a church to experience health and eventually growth, it must confirm why it exists. The purpose must be clarified, and the leadership and the congregation have to embrace it.

Go back to the story about Solid Ground Church. One of the first things Burt did to turn things around was to clarify the mission. He had to clarify the *why* before they could move forward with the *what* and *how*.

That's a key at this pivotal moment. Your tendency will gravitate to first focusing on the functions of the church—what the church should be doing—and the methods or systems for carrying out those functions. That's the how. For example, we all agree that ministries such as worship, fellowship, discipleship, evangelism, and prayer are primary functions of the church. But why do churches engage these functions? More important, why does *your* church engage those functions?

That's the heart of the challenge for churches stuck in life support. They have to go back to the beginning and clarify all over again why they exist. This foundation must be established before changes to functions and methods can take place. Don't get me wrong. You can't move from life support without changing your ministry strategy. That will come next. First, though, you have to begin by reestablishing the primary purpose of the church.

In revisiting your mission, my prayer is that you will go back to two key challenges that Jesus gave us all. The first can be found in Jesus's response to a question, "Which is the most important commandment?" He responded:

> "You must love the LORD your God with all your heart, all your soul, and all your mind." This is the first and greatest commandment. A second is equally important: "Love your neighbor as yourself." The entire law and all the demands of the prophets are based on these two commandments. (Matt. 22:37–40)

You can't go wrong if you design your church's mission around loving God and loving others. In fact, if you are fully committed to that, I believe you'll also address the second challenge Jesus gave to his disciples:

> Therefore, go and make disciples of all the nations, baptizing them in the name of the Father and the Son and the Holy Spirit. Teach these new disciples to obey all the commands I have given you. And be sure of this: I am with you always, even to the end of the age. (Matt. 28:19–20)

If you combine the greatest commandment with the Great Commission, I think you'll establish a great mission for your church. Then, if you can rally enough people around that mission, you have a foundation in place for the necessary changes that must follow for the church to return to health.

Here are some examples of mission statements from churches with whom I've served through consulting:

> "Helping people find and follow Jesus."
> —WESTSIDE COMMUNITY CHURCH
> IN BEAVERTON, OREGON

> "We connect people to a life-changing relationship with Jesus Christ."
> —VAN DYKE CHURCH IN LUTZ, FLORIDA

> "We exist to bring people one step closer to God, to each other, and to freedom in Christ."
> —THE CHAPEL IN SANDUSKY, OHIO

> "Our mission is to make disciples of Jesus Christ for the hope of the world."
> —FRAZER UNITED METHODIST CHURCH
> IN MONTGOMERY, ALABAMA

As you can see, there are many ways to share the same basic message. At the foundation of each of these statements, though, is a commitment to helping people love God, love others, and make disciples of Jesus Christ. Once enough of the influencers in your church can agree on and genuinely embrace a mission that reflects the heart of Jesus, you are prepared to take the next step, which is to initiate a change in vision and strategy.

Go Back to the Start: It's Time to Relaunch a New Life Cycle

Let me say it straight: If you agree that your church is now in the life support phase of the life cycle, then you really only have two options. First, you can proceed as you have been. If you do, the odds are good you'll have the same results. Because of that, it's very likely your church is going to eventually die and close its doors. The second option is that you do something that helps your church experience a new beginning. You need to start a brand-new life cycle.

I would argue that you have nothing to lose at this point. Why not make a bold move and relaunch the church? There may be some people in the church who aren't going to budge. They'd rather the church die than make any changes. If that's the case, chart a new course and challenge them to join. God may change their heart through the process. If not, encourage them to find another church that meets their needs. Don't let negative people who are focused on their own preferences impede you from helping the church become the church God wants it to be.

I know, from personal experience, that any time I've wanted a new level of health and strength in my life, I've had to engage some new disciplines. I had to have enough "want to" first, and then I needed to put a plan in place and work that plan to ultimately achieve my goal. I've never just drifted into a new place of health.

If I want to be a better golfer, then I have to practice my swing.

If I want to lower my blood pressure, then I have to eat better and exercise. If I want to attain more knowledge, then I have to read and study. If I want to experience health in my marriage, then I have to take the initiative to talk with my wife and set aside time with her. In all of these areas, if I want certain results, then I have to embrace a new vision and a new strategy to experience a change.

I'm always amazed, though, at how many churches want new health and growth but are not willing to embrace a new vision and strategy. They aren't willing to set aside traditions and current methods. They hold on to their same structures, strategies, and ministries and then pray that God will somehow miraculously intervene. We are stewards of God's mission. If we neglect our role in this mission, I think it's highly unlikely God will move. Dead plants don't produce fruit. Neither do dead churches.

So don't let negative people who are stuck to their ways hold your ministry hostage. If the church is facing an imminent death, it's time for a radical change. What do you have to lose?

With that, let me offer three options for you to move the church from life support to a relaunch. Some of these options are harder than others. You might decide to try one, and if it doesn't work, you can try one of the other options. Let me start with the least invasive option first.

Fire Yourselves

Imagine that your entire leadership team has been removed and a new team is going to start. Before you pack up your boxes and move everything out, take a moment to write down the key issues you've never tackled and the changes you wanted to make. Help the new leadership understand what's working, what's broken, and what's missing. Communicate the new initiatives they need to tackle and the things the ministry needs to stop doing.

Once the departing team has confirmed that new direction, become the new leadership team. Start over, but this time follow through with everything you just agreed to do when you were out of a job.

The reason this exercise is so helpful is that it helps to remove the emotions connected with core issues and new initiatives. It also eliminates the investment in ministries or strategies you've engaged in the past that aren't working. A new leadership team wouldn't have those attachments. They would start fresh. That's what you need to do as well.

More specifically, you also have to do the hard work of not only establishing a new mission statement but also rebooting everything. That means you'll have a clean slate to clarify a new vision for the future, new team values, and a new ministry strategy to reach new people. Within that new strategy, you'll need to relaunch your worship services, discipleship path, and evangelism efforts. Everything needs a new beginning.

For you to have success in this process, I encourage you to find an outside facilitator to navigate these conversations and help your team make good decisions about the future. Obviously, this is a service that The Unstuck Group offers to churches, but there are other organizations that can help as well. You will need that outside perspective to help you move forward. Speaking of outsiders, that brings me to the second option.

Hire a New Pastor

And give that person appropriate authority to initiate changes. More likely than not, it's going to be difficult for a team that's been a part of the ministry for years to make the changes required to generate a new start. You may very well need a new leader from outside the church to help you experience a new launch.

If you take this approach, though, you can't force the new pastor to operate within current structures and ministry strategies. You still need to go through everything I've just mentioned in the scenario where you fired yourselves. Only, this option brings the advantage of a new perspective to the team. This is even better than having a facilitator who would be with you for the planning but wouldn't be around to execute the change. You'll have someone on the team with fresh insights and experiences to put the plan into action.

The key will be giving up control. Your current staff and lay leadership team needs to give this new leader the freedom to chart a new direction. One good way to begin moving in this direction is to hire an executive search firm to find this new pastor. Though the board will ultimately make the final call on who is hired, giving the hiring process to an outside entity will help the board learn how to release control of every decision. More important, an outside search firm has far more expertise in finding the right match for a given situation.

Give the Keys to Another Church

At some point a conversation needs to happen around the stewardship of God's resources. If your church owns its facilities, you have an asset that the right church could use for kingdom impact. Either they could relaunch ministry in that location or they could sell the property and reinvest the resources in ministry initiatives. Either way, it would be much better for those resources to be used in a way that's producing fruit. Let's get those resources back in the hands of a church that's moving toward or experiencing sustained health.

One scenario that could be viable in today's ministry environment is that your building could potentially become a campus for an existing church. Many of the largest and fastest growing churches in the country are engaging a multisite strategy. In other words, they are one church meeting in multiple locations. If your church is dying, why not initiate a conversation with the healthiest church in your region and determine whether or not your building might become a campus of that church?

But beware. If I were the church on the receiving end of your building, there would be many strings attached. Remember, your church needs a new start. You can't give your building to a healthy church and expect them to hold on to the same ministries and methods that have led you to life support. Because of that, the healthiest scenario would be for your church to close for a season and then reopen as the new church. It would have a new mission, vision, and strategy. It would have new leaders. With that, you would be moving a church from death to new life. That would be a huge win for the kingdom!

There may be other options available to you, but I want you to catch the spirit of what I'm saying. You need to make radical changes. The ministry has to look different than it does today. For the churches willing to make these huge sacrifices, though, the potential exists to begin a new journey up the life cycle toward sustained health.

Experience Hope: But Develop a Plan and Put It into Action

I'm living in conflict right now. On the one hand, I want you to experience hope. After all, Jesus is the hope of the world. As Christ followers, we should embrace that. We're on a mission from God, and God has promised he will build the church. No matter the condition of the particular church you serve, God's going to build the greater church, and not even the powers of hell will be able to stop him. You're on the winning team. You should have hope.

On the other hand, you need to know that hope is not a strategy. You need a strategy.

I first came across that thought from Dr. Henry Cloud's book *Necessary Endings*. He described that sense of hopelessness we feel when we've tried every strategy possible to turn things around with an employee who just isn't cutting it. We can provide coaching. We can give them time and encouragement. We can't make them change. Eventually we get to the point where we desire for them to become a healthy, productive employee. But then we lose hope because we have no objective reason to expect anything will change.

That's when Cloud acknowledged, "Hope is not a strategy." He added, "This kind of hope is not worth spending more time and resources on. It is only buying you the time to continue to make more mistakes. If you are in a hole, rule number one is to stop digging."[2]

If your church is declining to the point that it's on life support, your first step is to stop digging. Engaging the same strategy that has gotten you to this point and hoping for different results is not going to work. You need a different strategy.

On that note, consider the following verse:

> But generous people plan to do what is generous,
>   and they stand firm in their generosity.
>   (ISA. 32:8)

I love that verse on many different levels. The most obvious is that it calls us to generosity. I want to be generous with my life. With everything that God has given me, I want to be the best steward possible so that God is honored. I believe generosity is one of the truest forms of worship.

The verse also highlights a principle that shapes how we should steward our resources. It suggests that people who are already generous plan to be generous and then stand firm in their generosity. In other words, they live out that plan without wavering. They are generous. They plan. They live it out.

I've seen that same pattern with churches pursuing sustained health. Healthy churches plan to do what is healthy and then put that plan into action. There's almost a tenacious focus on making sure nothing gets in the way of their being the healthy church they believe God has called them to be. They are healthy. They plan. They live it out.

For the churches stuck in life support, the current plan is clearly not working. It needs to change. A new pattern needs to be established.

I've found that some churches get stuck here because they fail to get perspective. They are afraid to acknowledge their current condition. If that's your church, I hope you find someone from outside your congregation who will be honest with your church, including its leadership. You need that clear understanding of your current reality before you'll be in a position to move forward.

Some churches are stuck here because they fail to plan. They assume if they hope and pray for a better future, they can cling to past practices and still find success. If that's your church, you need to eventually acknowledge that hope is not a strategy. Hope will not win people to Jesus. Hope will not grow people in their faith. Hope will not grow your church. You need a new plan.

Some churches are stuck here because they don't put the plan into action. They are unwilling to do the hard work of being disciplined and monitoring their progress. They spend a focused amount of time building a plan for the future, but then that plan gets stuck on a shelf someplace and fades from memory. If you aren't intentional about putting the plan into action, then you will naturally drift back into doing what you've always done. You will never drift to health. You need to put the plan into action.

Where do you tend to get stuck? Is it with perspective? Identify someone to facilitate a conversation with your team so you can define reality. Are you stuck with planning? Bring a team together to clarify your mission, vision, and strategy. Confirm who it is you're trying to reach, and then develop a plan to see that become reality. Are you stuck with putting the plan into action? Develop an intentional system for accountability. This is where you need others around you to make sure the follow-through actually happens.

Embrace the hope you have in Jesus, but remember that hope is not a strategy. Healthy churches plan for health and then put that plan into action.

In this final chapter, I talked about embracing a new mission, relaunching the ministry, and putting a new strategy in motion. What got the church to life support will not make it healthy again. That's why it's all about becoming new again. It really is time for God to begin a new work. Are you willing to join him in that mission?

CONCLUSION
Parting Words

One of my favorite Bible stories is Joshua's leading the nation of Israel into the promised land. In many ways, there are so many parallels to churches that get stuck. For forty years, the people of Israel were stuck. They grumbled. They complained. They wanted to go back to where they came from. Does this sound familiar? Then eventually Joshua took charge and led the nation to a place where only the Jordan River stood between them and the promised land.

At this point, Joshua didn't call a board meeting. He didn't take a vote. He didn't wait for unanimous consensus. He didn't wait for the complainers to stop grumbling. Instead, Joshua talked with God. It's at that point that God reassured him that the people of Israel would receive the land that was promised. Then God told Joshua:

> Today I will begin to make you a great leader in the eyes of all the Israelites. They will know that I am with you, just as I was with Moses. Give this command to the priests who carry the Ark of the Covenant: "When you reach the banks of the Jordan River, take a few steps into the river and stop there." (Josh. 3:7–8)

We know the rest of the story. Though the river was overflowing, the priests took that first step into the water and God moved. The raging waters stopped flowing and the riverbed became dry. The Israelites crossed on dry land. That's epic! I love that story!

But it's more than just a story; it's a model for how we should lead the church. We need to pray. We need to take our challenges to God and listen for him to direct our steps. We have to discover his vision for the future. We need to confirm the next steps he wants us to take. And then we need to act. Let me say that again: and then we need to act.

The story would have ended very differently if Joshua had decided to just keep praying. There would have been a very different outcome if Joshua had just waited for God to do something. That wasn't God's plan. God's plan was for Joshua and the Israelites to take the first step into the river. Once they put their faith in action and took that next step, God moved.

That same pattern works today. Start with prayer, and then act on God's plan. God's plan is not to go backward. God's plan is not to complain about the present situation. God's plan is for us to experience the land he's promised us. If we pray that God will reveal where he wants us to go and what we need to do next in order to get there, I'm confident God will answer that prayer.

LIFE CYCLES
Where Is Your Church?

Launch

Priority Focus: Reach new people.

General Characteristics: There's a fresh purpose. Leaders have big dreams for the future. Hope prevails. People gravitate to new things.

Foundations: Mission

Leadership: Rely heavily on volunteer leaders.

Ministry Strategy: Weekend services are the focus.

Systems: Few, if any, rules are implemented, and everyone is involved in almost every decision.

Staffing and Structure: Pastor and limited part-time staff.

Finances: New people don't give, so finances are tight.

> **Key Next Steps:** Connect people to the mission and give ministry away.

Momentum Growth

Priority Focus: Make space for new people—both physical space and ministry space.

General Characteristics: Entrepreneurial leaders gravitate to the team. People are united. Creativity is valued. There's an inviting culture: "Come and see." There's lots of buzz!

Foundations: Visions and values

Leadership: Typically personality-driven.

Ministry Strategy: New programming added to help people connect and take their next steps.

Systems: Leaders generally avoid establishing policies and systems.

Staffing and Structure: Ministry leaders added to start building teams.

Finances: New Christians don't give. Numerical growth generates financial growth, but not at the same pace.

> **Key Next Steps:** Confirm the vision for the future and give leadership away.

Strategic Growth

Priority Focus: Establish healthy strategy and systems.

General Characteristics: Outsiders would describe the team as high-performing. Leaders are still willing to change. The organization is more intentional.

Foundations: Strategy and systems

Leadership: Team-based leadership.

Ministry Strategy: The ministry strategy is focused around growth engines.

Systems: Growth necessitates establishing systems to keep everyone aligned.

Staffing and Structure: Administrative functions added. Staff empowered to lead their ministries.

Finances: Begin to build financial and giving systems to fund ministry and expand vision.

Key Next Steps: Clarify growth engines and develop systems and structure around that strategy.

Sustained Health

Priority Focus: Reproduce at all levels.

General Characteristics: The culture is collaborative. There's a focused vision and strategy. The leaders will take calculated risks. A balance exists between refreshed vision and healthy systems.

Foundations: Leadership development

Leadership: Empowered leaders and teams.

Ministry Strategy: Ministry programming is reproduced through multiple locations or services.

Systems: Healthy systems lead to empowered leaders and teams.

Staffing and Structure: Staffing and structure around growth engines, including multisite and/or church planting.

Finances: Stewardship and generosity culture in place; investing in reproducing the church.

Key Next Steps: Become a reproducing church with an intentional strategy for leadership and spiritual development.

Maintenance

Priority Focus: Keep people happy.

General Characteristics: Complexity reigns. There's a shift toward an inward focus. Leaders control. Traditions are protected. Growth is still happening, though at a slower pace. The vision stales.

Foundations: Programs and events

Leadership: Staff-driven with reduced volunteer empowerment.

Ministry Strategy: New ministry programming continues to expand and increase complexity with many events on the calendar.

Systems: Systems and methods begin to supersede the mission and vision.

Staffing and Structure: Ministry silos and overstaffing while finances remain strong.

Finances: May be the most financially healthy season for the church. Growth slows, but finances may continue to increase.

Key Next Steps: Revisit the staff leadership and refresh the vision. Get refocused and remove complexity.

Preservation

Priority Focus: Keep people from leaving.

General Characteristics: People desire to return to the "good old days." There's an unwillingness to change. Leaders blame other churches for decline. Division takes root. People and money begin to leave.

Foundations: Problems

Leadership: Board-driven.

Ministry Strategy: Ministries jockey to preserve their turf even as the church declines.

Systems: Culture becomes very bureaucratic. "What do the bylaws and constitution say?"

Staffing and Structure: Turf wars firmly established as staffing reductions offset financial decline.

Finances: Finances start to decline. Well-funded ministries (large reserves/endowments) can live here a long time.

Key Next Steps: Hire and empower new leadership to implement a fresh vision and a turnaround strategy.

Life Support

Priority Focus: Reach new people with old methods.

General Characteristics: The church is bleeding both people and money. The last remnant of leaders is holding on. Endowments keep churches like this open for many years.

Foundations: Crisis.

Leadership: Key family-or key donor-driven.

Ministry Strategy: Everything becomes focused on keeping the doors open.

Systems: Broken systems hasten ministry decline.

Staffing and Structure: Most paid positions eliminated with declining team morale.

Finances: Financial crisis usually is the primary trigger for a church to recognize the ministry is on life-support.

Key Next Steps: Close and relaunch or find another ministry to acquire the dying church.

Help for Getting Your Church Unstuck

If you'd like to have assistance identifying where your church is on the life cycle and get the help you need to move toward sustained health, The Unstuck Group helps churches by walking them through a four-step process:

1. **Assessment Phase: How are we doing?** You gain perspective and clarity on the health of your ministry and your position on the life cycle. You begin identifying opportunities for next steps.

2. **Strategy Phase: Where are we going?** You clarify your mission, vision, and core strategies and prioritize specific actions to get things moving.

3. **Structure Phase: Who does what?** We help you determine the best organizational structure to support your vision and future growth while getting the right people in the right roles.

4. **Action Phase: Are we seeing change?** We stick with you as you lead change, build momentum, monitor ministry health, and refresh your plans over time. We help you experience sustained health.

Our services are right-sized for churches regardless of attendance, locations, and denominations. If you'd like coaching to help you engage the solutions in this book, contact us by visiting TheUnstuckGroup.com or by calling 888.4UNSTUCK.

NOTES

INTRODUCTION

1. Aubrey Malphurs, *Advanced Strategic Planning: A 21st-Century Model for Church and Ministry Leaders*, 3rd ed. (Grand Rapids, MI: Baker Books, 2005, 2013), 10.

2. Les McKeown, *Predictable Success: Getting Your Organization on the Growth Track—and Keeping It There* (Austin, TX: Greenleaf Book Group, 2014), 19.

CHAPTER 1: LAUNCH

1. Ed Stetzer, "Equipping Church Planters for Success," *Enrichment Journal* (21 August 2009), http://enrichmentjournal.ag.org/200904/200904_036 _equipping.cfm.

2. Glenn Llopis, "The Content You Read Shapes How You Lead: Top 10 Leadership Themes," *Forbes* (18 November 2013), http://www.forbes.com /sites/glennllopis/2013/11/18/the-content-you-read-shapes-how-you-lead -top-10-leadership-themes/#!.

3. Yuyu Chen, "Nielsen: Younger Consumers are Easier to Reach Online," *ClickZ* (30 September 2013), http://www.clickz.com/clickz/news/2297713 /nielsen-younger-consumers-are-easier-to-reach-online.

4. The Unstuck Group interview with Todd Lollis.

CHAPTER 2: MOMENTUM GROWTH

1. Patrick M. Lencioni, *The Advantage: Why Organizational Health Trumps Everything Else in Business* (San Francisco: Josey-Bass, a Wiley Imprint, 2012), 97.

2. John Ortberg, *Soul Keeping: Caring for the Most Important Part of You* (Grand Rapids, MI: Zondervan, 2014), 89.

3. Lance Witt, *Replenish: Leading from a Healthy Soul* (Grand Rapids, MI: Baker Books, 2011), 25.

CHAPTER 3: STRATEGIC GROWTH

1. Tony Morgan, *Stuck in a Funk?* (Dallas, GA: Tony Morgan Live, LLC, 2013).
2. Michael E. Gerber, *The E-Myth Revisited: Why Most Small Businesses Don't Work and What to Do About It* (New York: HarperCollins, 2001), 4.
3. Greg Hawkins and Cally Parkinson, *Move: What 1,000 Churches Reveal About Spiritual Growth* (Grand Rapids, MI: Zondervan, 2011).
4. Ibid., 211–12.

CHAPTER 4: SUSTAINED HEALTH

1. Rick Warren, "Forget Church Growth, Aim for Church Health," *Pastors Community* (20 May 2016), http://pastors.com/health-not-growth/.
2. Texas Association of Counties, "Wise County Profile," *The County Information Program* (2015), http://www.txcip.org/tac/census/profile.php?FIPS=48497.
3. Association of Statisticians of American Religious Bodies, "County Membership Report: Wise County, Texas," *Association of Religion Data Archives* (2010), http://www.thearda.com/rcms2010/r/c/48/rcms2010_48497_county_name_2010.asp.
4. Ibid., 1990 Report. http://www.thearda.com/rcms2010/r/c/48/rcms2010_48497_county_name_1990.asp.
5. Association of Statisticians of American Religious Bodies, "County Membership Report: Paulding Country, Georgia," *Association of Religion Data Archives* (2010), http://www.thearda.com/rcms2010/r/c/13/rcms2010_13223_county_name_2010.asp.

CHAPTER 5: MAINTENANCE

1. Jason Fried and David Heinemeier Hansson, *Rework* (New York: Crown Business, 2010), 156.
2. Greg Hawkins and Cally Parkinson, *Move: What 1,000 Churches Reveal About Spiritual Growth* (Grand Rapids, MI: Zondervan, 2011), 25.

CHAPTER 6: PRESERVATION

1. Author interview with Ike Reighard, August 3, 2016.

CHAPTER 7: LIFE SUPPORT

1. Religious Bodies, "County Membership Report: Sussex County, Delaware," *Association of Religion Data Archives* (2010), http://www.thearda.com/rcms2010/r/c/10/rcms2010_10005_county_name_2010.asp.
2. Henry Cloud, *Necessary Endings* (New York: HarperBusiness, 2011), 89.

ABOUT THE AUTHOR

 **Tony Morgan** is founder and lead strategist of The Unstuck Group, a company that helps churches get unstuck through consulting and coaching experiences designed to focus vision, strategy, and action. He's written several books as well as articles that have been featured with the Willow Creek Association, Catalyst, and Pastors.com. He writes about leadership and strategy regularly at tonymorganlive.com.

Prior to starting The Unstuck Group, Tony was a pastor and served on the senior leadership teams at West Ridge Church in Georgia, NewSpring Church in South Carolina, and Granger Community Church in Indiana. Before full-time ministry, he served for approximately ten years in various local government roles, including a position as a city manager in Michigan, where he led a team of 150 people and oversaw a $20-million budget.

Tony lives near Atlanta, though his heart is still in Cleveland, Ohio, where his family has its roots. He's been married to Emily for more than twenty-five years, and they have four kids: Kayla, Jacob, Abby, and Brooke.

To learn more about Tony and The Unstuck Group, visit TheUnstuckGroup.com.